THE PULLOUT SELLOUT

The Betrayal of Afghanistan and America's 9/11 Legacy

SÉAMUS Ó FIANGHUSA (FENNESSY)
IM ÚR BLASTA

Copyright © 2021 by Séamus Ó Fianghusa (Fennessy)
THE PULLOUT SELLOUT
The Betrayal of Afghanistan and America's 9/11 Legacy
All rights reserved. No part of this book may be reproduced or used in any manner without written permission of the copyright owner except for attributed use of quotations.

Published by Im Úr Blasta, LLC.
Old Bridge, NJ.

Library of Congress Control Number: 2021922497
ISBN 978-1-7369229-5-8 (hardcover)
ISBN 978-1-7369229-4-1 (paperback)
ISBN 978-1-7369229-3-4 (ebook)

Cover art by Pixel Clan
Cover design by Séamus Ó Fianghusa (Fennessy)
www.imurblasta.com

DISCLAIMER

The views I express in this book are exclusively my own; I do not represent any entity, whether a group or an individual, in government or in the private sector. I freely mention and quote many people whom I have read, listened to, or watched, or have had productive discussions with, and who have said certain key things I have found to be poignant and relevant to the truthful message of this book. However, I do not in any way claim or imply that by mentioning their names that they are in lockstep with my opinions.
My take is entirely my own, and I take full and complete responsibility for any inaccuracies, mistakes, or controversial views.

**In Honor of our Patriot Dead,
2001/09/11 – 2021/09/11**

TABLE OF CONTENTS

ACKNOWLEDGMENTS 1

0. GET READY FOR A "HOT WASH" 6

I. THE GREAT SABOTAGE 37

II. THE ESTABLISHMENT'S RESPONSE 88

III. WHY EVERY AMERICAN SHOULD BE CONCERNED 137

IV. THOUGHTS ON THE FUTURE – THE SILVER LINING 194

POSTSCRIPT 248

APPENDIX A 253

APPENDIX B 258

SELECT BIBLIOGRAPHY 261

MORE INFO: IM ÚR BLASTA 264

MORE INFO: BRING K9 MATTIE HOME 267

MORE INFO: FREEDOM SUPPORT ALLIANCE 271

AUTHOR REVIEWS 273

ABOUT THE AUTHOR 275

ACKNOWLEDGMENTS

Even for an expeditious work such as this, a writer will be grateful to more people than he could ever properly thank, and so it is with this one. And I do apologize in advance to anyone who I might be leaving out here. By way of consolation, just know that more works are in the pipeline, and there will be that many more opportunities for me to express my personal thanks.

I feel I must start with Mike Figliola, author of the novel *The Slow Midnight on Cypress Avenue* and the upcoming *Fine is Flying Without You*. He has been so incredibly encouraging since the beginning of my public writing journey. Who knew back when we spent evenings sipping bubbly in Nunny's of Maspeth how Kerouac's spirit would lift us.

Bruce Crelin, author of *The Great War and the Golden Age of Hollywood Horror*, who has overlapping appreciations of faith, war, and entertainment. Garryowen in Glory!

Donald Vandergriff, author of *Adopting Mission Command: Developing Leaders for a Superior Command Culture* and other phenomenal works, has the wisdom and insight to help America's military out of its most pressing problems. He has been most helpful in developing my own deeper understanding of military affairs, as have the numerous distinguished members of our online group dedicated to developing for Mission Command.

And among these latter I must pay homage to the insightful contributions of Andrew Milburn, author of *When the Tempest Gathers*, and B.A. Friedman, author of *On Tactics*.

H. John Poole, author of *The Iwo Alamo*, who revolutionized my understanding of the importance of the details of tactical execution. He was also gracious enough to take a random call from me back when I was in Afghanistan. He has contributed greatly to this nation through widely sharing his wealth of military wisdom, and I am one of the grateful beneficiaries.

Pete Hegseth, author of *Modern Warriors*, with whom I had many conversations out on the range at Ft. Dix when we were both soldiers, and young; discussions that helped propel me in the direction I take today.

J.P. Lawrence, whose spectacular reporting for the venerable old *Stars and Stripes* set some wheels in motion.

Timothy J. Gordon, author of the recently released *The Case for Patriarchy*, I have gained tremendously from his thoughtful and faithful insight. *Deus Vult*.

Steven Mosher, author of *Bully of Asia*, I have gained knowledge from his sage perspective, and I am grateful that he took time to talk to me on these matters.

Jason Jones, co-author of *The Race to Save Our Century*, whose work on behalf of the vulnerable and exploited, including those in Afghanistan, is a genuine source of Gospel light.

My deeply honorable neighbors, the Kehoes, and the Chiangs; the LORD brings us together according to His will, and it's a beautiful thing.

Hekmat Ghawsi, once people know the full extent of his initiative, leadership, and bravery in service of both his countries, they will be in awe.

Andrew Squires, author of *Chasing the Taliban*; he was the first one to write a memoir out of the crew I went downrange with. He blazed a trail.

My brothers in arms (in no particular order!), Chad Paustian, Bryn Reynolds, Matt Higgins, Kevin Mulcahey, Jason Eaton, Larry Doane, Samuel Morris, Gary Keefer, Donald Loveland, Tom Burke, Brianna Puff, Greg

Papadatos, J.J. Falvey, Charles Sanders, Brendan Cooney, Christopher Daniels, Michael Schraeder, Michael Montgomery, Jason Pizzarello, Mark Tolley, and a whole host of others I cannot name because they are in sensitive positions on active duty.

To comrades on the other side, I pray eternal rest, eternal memory, Michael Tarlavsky, Justin Harris, Mike Cram, James "Woody" Wood, Hans Heck, Brian Fraker; and you brothers who I did not know before we lost you but who gave strength to my spirit, Christian Engeldrum, Wilfredo Urbina, Ryan Grady.

All the gallant heroes of the Fighting 69th and the Green Mountain Boys.

Do Chumann Thír Chonaill NuaEabhrac, i gcónaí dílis.

Do m'athair, mo Dhaid, an gaiscíoch is mó dá bhfuil ann.

Don bheirt mhac, nár rugadh, a chaill muid anuraidh ar Fhéile Dhul Isteach Mháthair Dé sa Teampall, an 21ú lá de mhí na Samhna; cuimhne shíoraí.

Agus do mo níon bheo, an banphrionsa Gaelach, Áine, Rós na Gaeilge. Is fá do choinnesa a ghním mo dhícheall.

THE PULLOUT SELLOUT

"*We praise the Almighty, the Ominpotent, who humiliated and defeated America, the head of disbelief.*

We praise Him for breaking America's back, tarnishing its global reputation and expelling it, disgraced and humiliated, from the Islamic land of Afghanistan."

– **Al Qaeda, 31 August 2021**

"*We succeeded in what we set out to do in Afghanistan.*"

– **President Biden, 31 August 2021**

0. GET READY FOR A "HOT WASH"

The way in which the United States pulled out of Afghanistan was disgraceful. Just in time for the 20th anniversary of the 9/11 terrorist attacks, it was a betrayal of those killed in the attacks, a betrayal of everyone who served and bled in the two decades afterwards, and a betrayal of our allies who placed their confidence and trust in us.

Indeed, the rushed and chaotic operation transformed a withdrawal into a retreat, and a retreat into a rout – a dishonorable end to the longest war in the history of the world's most powerful nation.

There might not have been any good end in store for the Afghan War, but couldn't the world's only superpower at least have done any better?

Of course it could have, and that is the real shock. This fiasco, the greatest military loss in American history, was self-inflicted. It was a voluntary defeat. One could even argue that it was a surrender.

GET READY FOR A "HOT WASH"

No other war in American history has ever ended like this, not even Vietnam.

The Pullout Sellout is an **immediate after-action review**, or "hot wash," of the Afghan debacle that marked the end of two decades of direct large-scale US troop involvement in foreign combat theaters following the terrorist attacks of September 11, 2001.

The people in power have a lot to lose if light continues to shine on their misdeeds. But they place their smug confidence in the fact that public memory is fleeting. There is an outburst of anger – here today, gone tomorrow, and the herd gets moved along.

But the end of the Afghan War is not just an episode of our history to be consigned to the past, a done deal meant to be stuffed away in our collective memory file. It is an ongoing tragedy on an epic scale.

THE PROBLEM

Here's the problem you and I face, and it's a deep problem. It's not just the events in Afghanistan itself. It's also that the establishment powers are on the verge of getting one over on us, the citizenry at large, because of the way that news cycles, public memory, and human psychology work.

Their manipulation of the public is contrary to basic decency.

Basic decency demands that the personhood of every human being is respected. This entails not treating average citizens as easily coerced suckers, but rather leveling with them when putting out public information.

Also, and obviously, it entails a respect for their very lives.

War is a grave matter. If we respect human life we do not send our forces to kill even an enemy unless it is absolutely necessary, never mind subjecting the brave members of our Armed Forces to unnecessary risk.

Well, if we read the situation simply on its face, it appears that the powers-that-be do not hold either the lives of our servicemembers or the lives of innocent civilians in much regard, nor do they respect the citizenry of the United States enough to be truthful with them.

As if getting conned were not bad enough, did you know that we in America are all **now in greater danger** because of how the United States and her allies pulled out from Afghanistan? American credibility trashed, Afghanistan a secure base for terrorists again, Communist China reaping a windfall of US military gear, to name only

GET READY FOR A "HOT WASH"

a few (some other big ones are named in the book, mostly in Section III).

And this situation was easily avoidable!

It all hinged on the manner in which the withdrawal was conducted, or rather, misconducted.

And so, the focus of this book is narrow: the specific series of events in 2021 that transformed a hazardous, unsteady stalemate in Afghanistan into a decisive victory for the Taliban and a humiliating defeat for the United States.

While I touch on some wider issues, the *way* the pullout happened and its consequences remain at the center – **not** whether we should have pulled out at all, or how long we should have stayed, or how messed up the past 20 years have been.

This cannot be emphasized enough. When the subject of Afghanistan is brought up, a typical sampling of comments might produce something like the following:

"We all knew it was going to fall apart anyways."

"Afghanistan had everything it needed to succeed, the failure is on them."

"Enough is enough! What are we accomplishing there after 20 years?"

"The U.S. armed and trained the predecessor of the Taliban, this is on America."

"What did you expect when you invade a country, set up a puppet government, and try to impose a foreign political system on them?"

"American ideas on counter-insurgency do not work."

"Osama bin Laden and his associates were from Saudi Arabia, not Afghanistan."

"It's the fault of [*insert some previous President's name here*]."

These comments are all taken from real conversations with people of diverse political opinions, and collectively they appear to be common reactions.

Those assertions, and ones like them, are being debated – and I'm sure they will continue to be, for many years to come – but they're not what this book is about.

And further, this book absolutely does not entertain the so-called "stabbed in the back myth" that was prevalent in certain circles of the American military after Vietnam, the French military after Algeria, and the German military after the Great War.

There were certainly a great many hypothetical forks in the road over the past two decades, so many opportunities to turn left or right. And there are a number of deeply embedded systemic issues which are non-hypothetical, which plague us right now, but which are beyond the scope of this book.

What *The Pullout Sellout* does is talk about a discreet period of time in the summer of 2021 when reasonable steps could have been taken, but were not taken, to ensure the Afghan withdrawal was truly "safe and orderly." It also discusses the catastrophic consequences, and possible ways of successfully dealing with the fallout.

What's at stake is the very peace, safety, and security of the United States, the lives and honor of American servicemembers, and the lives of innocent civilians, American, allied, and Afghan alike.

9/11 AND THE ANTI-9/11

We must put to rest the false assertion that the chaos of the Afghan withdrawal was the natural consequence of the act of leaving the country itself, rather than of the specific asinine decisions of the U.S. leadership.

Let's say there's a house and a fire starts and there's a family inside. And it turns into a raging inferno. 9-1-1 would be called and the fire department would come. What the firefighters do is fight the fire. They might disagree in their professional opinions on whether the fire can be put out, or whether the house is a lost cause that nothing can be done about and which should be abandoned.

But the one thing they would agree on is they would at least keep the fire at bay. At the very least they would do everything to fight the fire while they got the people out. They would not, they *absolutely would **not*** be saying, "Oh, you know what? The house is going anyways. We can't do anything about it. Let's stand outside and throw gasoline on it with the people still inside."

But that's analogically exactly what the US leadership did with regard to Afghanistan in the summer of 2021. It was the opposite of the strong, decisive leadership shown 20 years before in response to that other 9-1-1, September 11, 2001. (We're just talking about that day and the weeks immediately after the terrorist attacks – the wisdom of the leadership decisions made in the subsequent years is very much in question!).

In fact, let's extend the analogy to that fateful day. The Fire Department of New York (FDNY) did actually come to the disaster scene on 2001/09/11 when the 9-1-1 call came in. We know for a fact that they would have fought to the end to rescue people because they actually *did* so, and 343 of them lost their lives as a result, along with many other heroic emergency personnel.

At 8:46 AM, the North Tower was struck by the first plane. This was followed only 17 minutes later, at 9:03 AM, by the second plane striking the South Tower. Instantaneous death by incineration for hundreds, and many thousands of others put into the terror of their lives – 17,000 is one estimate of how many people were in the towers at the time, not including the many more people in the streets and the surrounding buildings.

The evacuation began immediately and proceeded with great speed. In less than an hour, at 9:59, the South Tower collapsed, ending the lives of everyone still trapped.

Imagine if, upon seeing that, the authorities decided the North Tower couldn't be saved either and immediately called off the rescue? Imagine they ordered the firefighters back, and blocked emergency personnel from going in to save anyone. Terrified civilians would be left to fend for themselves. And even worse, imagine they decided to help along the process of building collapse by setting off demolition explosives *with people still inside.*

As is turns out, the North Tower did collapse at 10:28. And the real-life heroes fought to save lives till the very last second.

But if the hypothetical scenario had actually happened, the consequences would be severe for the cowards responsible. Heads would roll, so to speak, and rightfully so. Every American with the slightest sense of right and wrong would naturally have been filled with disgust and contempt for such feckless leadership.

But that was not quite a hypothetical scenario. It is what *actually happened* in Afghanistan under the direction of the United States in the summer of 2021. Obviously not it the particular details, but in the substance. That is how the war that began on 9/11 of 2001 was concluded in 2021.

I cannot emphasize this more strongly: **If you understand the point of the analogy, you understand why the manner of withdrawal from Afghanistan was disgraceful.** And if you don't think it's such a big deal, then we have bigger problems than this book can deal with.

Just as one may speak of Christ and Antichrist, hero and antihero, so also there is 9/11 and **the anti-9/11:** the Afghan pullout, a dreadful, dystopian counterpart. The amazing bravery of those actually *doing* the work on the ground was the same. But the inverse image is appropriate for conceptualizing the *leadership* that succeeded in 2001, and culpably failed in 2021.

Let's look at some similarities and differences:

2001 – The start of the Global War on Terror (GWOT)

2021 – The end of a US troop commitment in the first foreign theater of GWOT, Afghanistan

2001 – Innocents attacked and murdered by Jihadist terrorists in the United States

2021 – Innocents abandoned by the United States to be attacked and murdered by Jihadist terrorists in Afghanistan

2001 – American civilians are innocent victims, Jihadists are the active agents of the terror attacks

2021 – American leadership are the active agents in engineering a catastrophe that leaves an untold number of innocent victims in its wake, Afghan, allied, and American alike

Despite the distinctions, 2001 and 2021 have this terrible quality in common:

2001 – In the aftermath of the 9/11 terrorist attacks, **Jihadists gloat in victory**

2021 – In the aftermath of the humiliating Afghan withdrawal, **Jihadists gloat in victory**

THE SOLUTION

Fortunately, there is a solution. And that solution is YOU, the American citizen, empowered with the knowledge, questions, and points of discussion in this book.

This intellectual ammunition does not consist of facts and figures per se; an internet search can turn up reams of that within seconds. It consists of a thought process, a way of viewing the overall situation with a rational clarity that cuts to the heart of the issue. We bypass the cognitive weed fields that are meant to distract and obfuscate.

You might already know a lot. Perhaps you were a professional, multi-deployment special operator. Or maybe you don't know much about military affairs, but you're a concerned American who has a gut feeling that what happened was just not right and you want to know more, to know better. Maybe you're not even an American but just a decent person who wants to get to the heart of the matter.

Any which way, this book will help edify and elucidate in the spirit of Thomas Paine's *Common Sense*.

For instance, when people talk about the "disaster in Afghanistan," *what does that actually mean?* It sounds a bit nebulous, can we flesh out the concept just a bit?

We can surely get incredibly detailed when giving an answer, but here's the catch: Can we *only* get detailed enough to succinctly and accurately summarize?

The thing is, there are many sources from which to get voluminous quantities of detail which will be of great value to the historian. Those who are so interested will do the follow up research. But at the foundational level of inquiry, everyone of sound mind wants to **get to the point.**

Some may delve further, others will stop there. But when we start off by getting to the point, we have a common base, a steady foundation upon which to build our own individual frames of reference.

This is crucial, because one of the great challenges in talking to people about the crisis is their level of awareness. Even those who are patriotic, are veterans, and are sympathetic to the plight of their fellow humans in distress often have not grasped the insane level of malfeasance that had to go into engineering the Afghan catastrophe, or how it adversely affects our daily lives at home.

Such a lack of awareness is partially a natural consequence of the genetically imposed limits of human attention – you can see the forest for the trees, and you can focus your sight on an individual tree, but you cannot focus on each individual tree simultaneously. But it is also an artificial consequence of the current top leadership (the President, the Secretary of Defense, certain Generals) skillfully "spinning."

I don't like the wool being pulled over my eyes by anybody. I am pretty sure you don't either.

Thankfully, we have each other's "six" – that's a military way of saying we have each other's back (based on imagining standing on a clockface; facing forward is twelve o'clock, so that facing back is six o' clock).

And so, this book aims to arm you with true, logical, and concise points of discussion to aid you in constructing your own mental frame of reference with regard to the great Afghan pullout disaster.

To demonstrate, take a look at the following misdeeds of the US leadership, which we will take a closer look at in Section I and intermittently throughout this book. Tell yourself if it doesn't look like they actively undermined their own troops. Whether they were knowingly doing so or not, the effect was the same.

As of June 1, 2021, there were some 2,500 US servicemembers in Afghanistan in support and advisory positions. The Taliban were on the move but the Afghan forces were fighting back hard. Yet, the United States leadership made specific and consecutive warfighting and policy decisions during the fateful summer which assisted the Taliban to complete victory. They:

1) Removed assets from Afghan forces (air, intel, logistical, etc.) which we had trained them to depend on for fighting – and then blamed the Afghans for not fighting!

2) Abandoned Bagram Airfield (the only strategic air base in the country) with great combat speed and efficiency, and without coordinating with the Afghan relief.

3) Voluntarily gave up – yes, *surrendered* – the capital city of Kabul to the Taliban - even when the enemy had offered not to contest American control.

4) Gave the Taliban the names of American civilians in the country and of Afghans who supported us.

5) Refused to allow US troops to leave the confines of Kabul Airport to conduct rescues.

A – Americans and Afghan friends were thus left to make it to the airport on their own, and at the mercy of the Taliban.

B – Thousands of US and allied troops were jam packed into a relatively small area to be sitting ducks for attacks.

C – When troops and civilians were inevitably killed, the US leadership retaliated with a deliberate precision strike that did not kill a single terrorist, but did kill several little children.

6) Ignored the counsel of allies in order to rush out of the country according to the timeline the Taliban ordered the US to follow.

7) Gave the Taliban unprecedented leverage over the U.S. and others through negligent abandonment of:

A - American citizens

B - Afghan allies

C - contract work dogs and rescue dogs

D - many billions of dollars worth of lethal and "sensitive item" arms and equipment

Wow. This is some heavy stuff.

CALL OF DUTY

As an American citizen, my conscience compels me to speak up. I cannot sit idly by while the debacle is buried and forgotten. There is too much at stake. I will not take this lying down, nor can I stomach the lying. Those responsible *must* be held ACCOUNTABLE.

It was absolutely gut wrenching to see the implosion of the American project in central Asia, and it's absolutely gut wrenching to see the aftermath. And for me, it's not something that is far off that I'm just watching on the news. I have had personal contact with people that are there on the ground in Kabul right now or who have family stuck there, and with others who were able to get out with great difficulty.

The fact that I have personal connections with the situation only means that some extra propellant was added to the mix of my internal motivational fuel. It does not make me special; not only are there many thousands of other concerned and involved veterans, but this is an issue of grave importance to all Americans, even if they have no military or Afghan connection whatsoever.

Caomh faoi mholadh, borb faoi mhaslú.

This is the Irish language motto of the military unit I am beyond honored to have served with for a decade, the New York National Guard's legendary Fighting 69th. The motto was adopted by the Regiment to express its own spirit, modeled off the august qualities of the Irish Wolfhound. I embrace its ethic as my own.

It translates as "Gentle when stroked, fierce when provoked."

And boy, the American upper leadership's incomprehensible misconduct of the pullout from the Afghan War was the most severe provocation *from our own side* I have yet seen in my lifetime. I would not be doing my duty as an American if I did not substantively respond to it.

There was initially a lot of information overload as events progressed rapidly in the summer of 2021, particularly in August. But once the enormity of the situation became clear to me, I became passionate about distilling it into its essentials in order to gain clarity of insight. I was also determined to share – since the Afghan debacle is a matter of grave public concern, I felt the burning call of duty to point out what's really going on to anybody who would listen.

Fortunately, many did listen, for a time.

During the peak of media attention to the Fall of Afghanistan in August and early September of 2021, I did a number of interviews which were very well received by so many veterans who were infuriated and saddened by the Afghan crisis.

I was initially interviewed by *Stars and Stripes*, and my comments, along with those of other veterans, resonated with enough people that they were reprinted in such outlets as *BBC News*, *Military.com*, the *New York Post*, and *Newsmax*.

From then, I was asked to do an interview for NBC's Today Show. The leadup caused a bit of buzz among people who knew me. One soldier named Sean, whose Squad Leader I used to be, gave me some heartwarming encouragement.

"**Tell 'em how we really feel**." Sean had developed into an excellent noncommissioned officer (NCO), a Sergeant. He knew me well enough to know I was up to the task.

"**That's my purpose, brother**," I replied.

The interview was recorded, edited, and aired. Of course, much of what I related was cut out. This is normal for anybody for television, such is the nature of the business. But I was very satisfied with what they did broadcast. So was a wide community of my brothers.

For instance, an old family friend who is in the active Army contacted his mother, who got the message through to me.

"Saw Jimmy [*as I used to be called*] on the Today Show this morning. **He clearly expressed how many of us feel**."

I kept the ball rolling for as long as I had it. The high point was an in-studio interview at the CNN headquarters in New York City. It was even more a matter of note at this point, because the COVID pandemic was not long in the past and fewer guests were doing such live appearances.

The positive feedback was overwhelming. I continued to speak on various outlets – TV, podcasts, and radio shows – in both the US and Ireland, in both English and Irish, through early September.

But in the leadup to the 20th anniversary of the terrorist attacks of September 11, the demand for news on the debacle dried up.

Well, there are any number of reasons for why this was the case, but that was not going to deter me from getting this message out. I was determined, and remain

GET READY FOR A "HOT WASH"

determined, to make the call to "Never Forget" 9/11 and its aftermath into a living reality. This book is the result.

My mother is from Korea and spent some years of her childhood in the devastation of the war (1950-53). It was during this time that the Communists "disappeared" her father, my grandfather, who was never to be seen again. She is no military historian, but she knows the heroic name of Douglas MacArthur the way most Americans know (or used to know) George Washington and Abraham Lincoln.

MacArthur nearly obliterated North Korea at one point but was eventually fired by President Truman. Nevertheless, he is held in the highest regard by Koreans of my mother's generation; here was a general who knew it was his duty to win.

He was famous for making West Point's motto his personal credo: **DUTY, HONOR, COUNTRY.**

It is the spirit of this motto that animates *The Pullout Sellout*.

AN INFORMAL *AAR* (AFTER ACTION REVIEW)

In the infantry, the work of squads and platoons is the bread-and-butter of the fighting foot soldier's experience. (Squads are generally groups of 9-12 soldiers led by a junior sergeant who is a non-commissioned officer. Platoons are composed of 3-4 squads and are led by a senior non-commissioned officer as the Platoon Sergeant, who is paired with a junior commissioned officer, a Lieutenant, who is the Platoon Leader/Commander). After every mission, training exercise, and battle drill, we have an informal After Action Review (AAR) to assess and critique our performance with the goal of sustaining our strengths and improving on our weaknesses.

The informal AAR, or "hot wash," is to be distinguished from the formal After Action Review or Report. The latter is done after a thorough and comprehensive examination at a higher echelon of command.

I will use the term "hot wash" to avoid any confusion. In any case, an informal AAR/hot wash is what *The Pullout Sellout* is in relation to the end of America's Longest War.

The Wikipedia entry for "Hotwash" (it can be spelled as one word or two) has a link to a source which is surprisingly good at explaining the term, all the more surprising because the source is a Safe Schools newsletter, albeit one published by the U.S. Department of Defense. As such, I think it would be useful to give a big quote from it here:

Hot Wash: Clean Up and Cool Down After an Exercise

... a Hot Wash gathers the lessons learned during an exercise before they lose their immediacy for the participants.

The term Hot Wash comes from the practice used by some soldiers of dousing their weapons in extremely hot water as a means of removing grit and residue after firing. While this practice by no means eliminates the need to properly break down the weapon later for cleaning, it removes the major debris and ensures the cleaning process goes more smoothly. One infantry soldier described it as "the quick and dirty cleaning that can save a lot of time later."

The Hot Wash conversation serves much the same purpose. It does not replace the After Action Report (AAR) which can include a formal write-up, analysis, charts, and even slides. Rather, the Hot Wash prepares the team for the AAR. According to Tim Price, Installation Antiterrorism Officer, Fort Benning, "A Hot Wash is a conversation before the official AAR which captures events while they are still fresh on the participants' minds."

Here's what you'll get in the upcoming pages:

I. The Great Sabotage

Here we make clear that the incompetent, even *sinister* decisions of the upper-level US leadership engineered an unnecessary disgrace. Further, many of us saw it coming.

II. The Establishment's Response

President Biden's strongest speech on the Afghan War, given upon the removal of the last US troops, is assessed and analyzed. The flashlight of rational thought is pointed at it to reveal the true meaning and deeper implications of what lies under the rhetorical veneer.

III. Why Every American Should Be Concerned

Most Americans are totally against getting bogged down in foreign quagmires that produce no clear victory or benefit for us. But some Americans fail to distinguish between this and the catastrophic fruits of withdrawing in weakness – they think it doesn't matter, that we just need to focus on home.

Well, the botched withdrawal actually has everything to do with home and our safety, security, and way of life. Our great nation has been turned into a buffoonish embarrassment, with severe results for our veterans and our relations with other nations. Jihadist terrorists have been emboldened beyond measure. Communist China has moved into the vacuum created by America's self-imposed defeat, to the peril of all free peoples.

IV. Thoughts on the Future – The Silver Lining

Some things that need to be done, at a minimum, to come back from the brink.

The senior leadership who disgraced the United States must be held accountable – including President Biden himself. A look at what legally constitutes treason and if the President's malfeasance meets that standard. This is an extremely serious matter which must be approached, not with loose speculation, but with calm and rigorous discernment. Also:

- We must sustain what we do well (there is plenty).

- We must promote a culture of organized decentralization in order to achieve the best possible results for the common good. In the military sphere, this means "Mission Command."

- We must recognize America's internal weakness because of its stark political division, and only engage in foreign wars that can compensate for this vulnerability.

- We must embrace the Afghan American community. They bring much good and hope for the future to the already established citizenry of the United States.

At the end of each section, I have included a list of helpful articles as a starting point for further research. And at the end of the book is a bibliography of helpful books, also as a starting point for further research. As an appendix, I have included an outline summary of key points from *The Pullout Sellout*. Also, as a bonus appendix, I have included Gen. Douglas MacArthur's inspiring but hard to find speech to the Fighting Irish, New York's 69th Infantry Regiment, on the eve of America's active involvement in World War II.

THE PULLOUT SELLOUT GOES TO WASHINGTON

I guarantee that what you will get from *the Pullout Sellout*, if you digest its contents with an open mind and a willing heart, is mental clarity on this major issue of war and peace. The stirrings of the heart must pass through the filter of the mind and withstand the scrutiny of reason if they are to be of any value. I hope you would agree that the result here is honest and fresh.

However, I absolutely do not claim this work to be comprehensive. It is not the final word, but rather the opposite – it is a starting word.

I am not in the business of passing off unsupported assumptions as fact. If I make a bold assertion, I am also telling you why I make it. If I am telling you my impression or opinion on a matter, I will make clear that it's my impression or opinion.

As far as internal American politics, **this book is non-partisan.** I found it necessary to write this way in order to maintain the specificity of its scope – Just the Afghan withdrawal, ma'am. If criticism or praise is to be meted out, it is done so on the basis of the specific deeds being assessed and not because of the underlying political ideologies of the people doing the deeds.

However, I make no bones about the fact that my point of view is unabashedly American.

I take the perspective of James McKay Rorty, an American hero from my ancestral Irish county of Donegal. He was killed stopping Pickett's Charge at Gettysburg in 1863. He told his father that his higher motive for fighting was "attachment to, and veneration for the Constitution, which urged me to defend it at all risks." The Constitution of the United States of America deserves this attachment and veneration because it aims to "secure the Blessings of Liberty to ourselves and our Posterity." Those who protect that with their very lives deserve respect and gratitude.

As such, my loyalty to my brothers in arms is fierce – Armed Forces servicemembers' lives matter. I cannot sit idly by and let the farcical nature of the end of the Afghan War come and go without my public response, one that will stay on the record. History's judgment begins *now*.

The American fighter is a noble specimen of humanity because of the selfless sacrifice in the service of the common good which American military culture inculcates. The Armed Forces of the United States are built on a heritage of honor. *Honor* – that attribute which bears witness to a particular dignity. It is an enhanced dignity in the case of Soldiers, Sailors, Airmen, and Marines (joined now by the Guardians of the newly created Space Force). They deserve far better than the disgrace that was imposed on them on the eve of 9/11's 20th anniversary.

Everything I say in these pages is true, accurate, and researched. However, I make no pretense of being a distant and disinterested observer. I am an American combat veteran. This is personal.

On the other hand, I also make no pretense of having all the answers. That's not what a hot wash is for. Its value lies precisely in the fact that it was written so closely to the historical events it tries to extract some sense out of. This is a personal reflection, but one that is meant to be useful to my fellow citizens. *You do not have to read it in order; you can dip in and out at your leisure, it will be just as edifying.*

The book presents **the essential elements** of the Afghan withdrawal. By digesting its contents, I believe we will be in a better position to participate in the decision-making processes of our great Republic. The elites will not be able to pull the wool over our eyes – *THIS* is democracy in action.

Pursuant to this purpose, **The Pullout Sellout is being presented to members of both political parties in both the Senate and the House of Representatives of the United States Congress.** I invite you guys to reference it if you decide to contact your elected officials on this issue of existential consequence to the American nation. In fact, I encourage you to.

The goal of the book is for the regular citizen to be empowered, and the writing is structured to that end. Even though many of you are doubtlessly military or terrorism or Afghan specialists, I make the assumption that most of you are not. As such, I have strived to maintain a conversational tone, as if I were speaking to my neighbors (who are, by the way, intelligent and patriotic). I have kept military and technical jargon to a minimum, and what is included is explained.

I very consciously use the first person plurals "we," "us," "our," to refer to the United States of America and Americans. *We* are in this together.

That said, I wish to make clear that I do not profess to speak for all veterans; my views are my own. Nevertheless, I know for a fact, from innumerable personal interactions and online commentary, that a great many veterans, currently serving servicemembers, and concerned civilians agree with the views set forth on these pages.

Another part of the value of this book derives from the salient fact that I am just a regular dude. Yes, I am a combat veteran; I did my part and I did it well, but so did many hundreds of thousands of others. If the government and military establishment wants to mess around with our lives and sacrifices, they better convince the average GI Joe and Jane that it's worth it.

GET READY FOR A "HOT WASH"

Most people get it that there is government and military business that can't be made public. For instance, imagine if the raid that killed Osama bin Laden had been broadcast publicly beforehand; obviously, the end would have been different. But while most people take for granted that the specifics of particular operations have to be kept secret for everyone's safety, the rationale for the broad outlines of policy should be graspable to average Joe and Jane Citizen. Please spare me any talk about some elite expert knowing better.

If you actually do know better, the road forward to achieve triumph for your views is to convince people that you are correct by respecting their own ability to assess the evidence that you are putting before them. It is disrespectful and arrogant to claim an aloof superiority, where you can't be bothered to explain yourself honestly and non-condescendingly to those whom your policy is affecting. Elected and appointed officials, please take heed.

One of the most insightful books ever written on the primordial intellectual underpinnings of the United States is a work called *Catholic Republic: Why America Will Perish Without Rome*. In it, constitutional scholar and philosopher Timothy Gordon starts off with an introductory chapter called "An Introduction Important Enough to Be a Chapter."

Well, I have written something similar to that here. This has been a longer than average intro, but I hope you find that it has been worth it.

Let us honor the victims murdered on 9/11 of 2001, as well as the sacrifices of the brave American Soldiers, Sailors, Airmen, and Marines who have fought and bled since then. For their sake, I invite you to journey into *The Pullout Sellout: The Betrayal of Afghanistan and America's 9/11 Legacy.*

Let's do this. Let the Gaelic battle cry of the Fighting 69th ring in our mind's ear as we charge into the fray:

Fág an Bealach! "Clear the Way!"

I. THE GREAT SABOTAGE

"*It feels like not only a betrayal of what our soldiers have bled for, the way in which we're pulling out is something that's disgraceful.*" **– Séamus Fennessy on NBC's TODAY Show, 16 August, 2021**

In August of 2021, before the US and NATO completed their withdrawal from Afghanistan, I scribbled the following notes:

"Unless there is some miraculous change, the situation in Afghanistan on the 20th anniversary of the 9/11 terrorist attacks is shaping up to be the greatest military defeat in the history of the United States.

And it would be a voluntary defeat."

The miraculous change never came.

The enemies of the United States and of all civilized nations – the Taliban and groups like them – never defeated American or other NATO forces in battle. Yet, they emerged as the victors.

This is because they succeeded in their war aims, while we failed at ours. We failed to achieve even the modified and minimized war aims put in place to save face when it became clear that the US would never attain the simple option of total victory.

Americans have been sacrificed in the cataclysmic conflict with Islamist Jihadism at least since September 11, 2001. Yes, there was much that happened before that day, but that day was a turning point in the collective mentality of the American people. The mass murder of some 3,000 innocent people spurred the civilized world to fury. "Never forget" was the cry that echoed across the North American continent and the globe.

Exactly 20 years later, on the very eve of the anniversary, America had a choice to exit Afghanistan with strength.

Instead, she exited in a manner so inexplicable in its consistent sequence of incompetent decisions that an observer could be forgiven for assuming that the US government was working on the side of the Taliban/Al Qaida/Islamic State.

As the events were unfolding in mid-2021, it was somewhat unclear where all the bad decisions were coming from. And while there are still questions to be answered, it is increasingly clear that they came from the top, right from the place where the buck stops – and starts.

Why Would Afghanistan Be Our Greatest Defeat?

Afghanistan is America's greatest military defeat, ever.

This is a bold statement, couched in awfully strong language. But is it hyperbole or a serious claim? And if it is a serious claim, on what basis can we make this assertion?

The answer is elegant in its simplicity. Here it is: Because the enemy has conquered the disputed territory *while our troops are still in the disputed territory.*

This has **never** happened in the history of the American Republic, until now.

One may rebut this assertion by pointing out that the US was defeated by the British in New York in 1776, or by the Germans at the Kasserine Pass in 1943, or any number of other American losses. But these all involved battles or campaigns, not entire wars.

Historically, America just did not lose wars. The only contender for the loss column in early American history was the War of 1812 (which lasted until 1815).

However, this armed conflict against the United Kingdom is typically seen as a stalemate, a tie.

After World War II, it's a different story. Aside from short and victorious interventions (Grenada, Panama, the Gulf War), we have had several multi-year wars from 1945 onwards – Korea, Vietnam, Iraq, Afghanistan. And *not a single one of these* has resulted in a decisive victory for the United States. This is particularly ironic given that the US did not have the post-WWII status of a spent imperial power that had already seen its glory days come and go, but rather was the world's new most powerful nation and the ostensible guarantor of freedom and democracy to those with whom she was allied.

And yet, success in these multi-year wars has been either nonexistent or comparatively minimal. Korea and Iraq would perhaps most accurately be seen as a stalemate and a Pyrrhic victory, respectively. The Republic of Korea (the South) has turned out quite well and is a source of hope. But the Democratic People's Republic of Korea (the North) is quite the opposite – it is a humanitarian nightmare and an international nuisance even two-thirds of a century after the informal end of the Korean War in 1953. As far as Iraq, it's too soon to see what will eventually become of it. But speaking for myself, as it stands right now, I wouldn't exactly want to take my family on a vacation there.

As far as flat-out losses, there is only Vietnam and Afghanistan. Vietnam certainly involved larger American numbers in terms of servicemembers deployed as well as of total casualties. But, the overt American involvement in the war ended with a negotiated settlement, the Paris Peace Accords of January, 1973. The situation was essentially another stalemate, not identical to Korea, but similar to it. Not until two years later, in 1975, did Communist North Vietnam launch the offensive that would conquer the free Republic of (South) Vietnam.

The US was not defeated on the battlefield, but it counts as a lost war because the American goal of keeping South Vietnam free of Communist rule failed, whereas the enemy succeeded in their goal of reunifying Vietnam on their own terms.

"MODICUM OF SUCCESS"

2021's chaotic pullout from Afghanistan is now a historical fact. It happened. And it truly does feel like a betrayal. I feel this way for good reason. So much has been invested in life and limb and blood of Americans and of our allied coalition partners. And of course, the Afghans themselves have sacrificed so much to keep the Taliban at bay.

What on earth did we accomplish there?

General Mark Milley, the Chairman of the Joint Chiefs of Staff (the highest military position possible) gave a candid assessment that we had achieved a strategic stalemate, a "modicum of success." This was before the final Taliban offensive.

For all that we had invested over two decades, in money, sweat, and blood, achieving only a "modicum of success" was rather underwhelming. But because it was bought at such a high price, and was preventing the emergence of further evils, what little that was accomplished was worth preserving.

Initially, the invasion was to punish the perpetrators of the 9/11 attacks. Of course, everyone wanted to get Osama bin Laden, but that was never the major objective by itself. Al-Qaeda and the Taliban were to be destroyed. Yes, we were there to remove the Taliban from power because they gave safe haven to and supported Al Qaeda, but the idea was to remove them permanently. Ideally it would have been the elimination and destruction of the Taliban – their complete annihilation.

And then the radical Jihadist government was to be replaced with a Western-style democratic republic. Right? Well, that was never going to happen, despite our best efforts.

Nobody envisioned that the United States would be fighting for decades to come. And in fact, we ceased active combat operations in 2014. We were seven years past that when the country fell. The troops that we had there were just a backup for the Afghans; nevertheless, we did have troops there and, as President Trump had pointed out, it was costing us about fifty billion dollars a year – nearly the price of Russia's *entire* military budget. Nobody envisioned or wanted us to stay fighting in perpetuity, or have that kind of burden in perpetuity.

Nevertheless, it was in America's vital national interest to prevent total disaster. But in fact, we promoted total disaster in the summer of 2021 better than the enemy ever could have. Instead of just dimming the lights, we tore the plug right out of the wall, along with the socket.

A VERY *VERY* SHORT HISTORY OF THE WARS

I'm not going to delve too much at all into the history of the GWOT or of the countries involved; there is too much easily available info out there to make that a worthwhile venture for a work of bounded focus such as this. However, I will touch on a few very basic points so we can go forward with some common context.

The Global War on Terror began on September 11, 2001, with the terrorist attacks on New York City, the Pentagon near Washington, D.C., and rural Pennsylvania. The first foreign theater of the war was Afghanistan, which a US-led coalition invaded shortly thereafter. The single largest theater of the war was Iraq, which a US-led coalition invaded in March of 2003. Each of these specific theaters are typically referred to as individual wars in their own right. There have been and currently are other areas in which US forces operate in various capacities for the GWOT; for instance, Mali, Djibouti, and the Philippines. However, the centerpieces of troop commitments were to Iraq and Afghanistan.

The wars in both these countries started in a similar way – with a bang, with a big invasion. However, the manner each invasion was conducted was quite different. In Afghanistan, it was done with the minimum of troops – about 2,500 in country by December of 2001. Iraq, on the other hand, was invaded with nearly 200,000 US troops. The result achieved was the same in both cases. Both invasions resulted in swift and overwhelming military victories for the United States and its allies.

Concerning the pattern of troop strength in those countries during the wars, Afghanistan resembles the pattern of Vietnam, where there was an escalation gradually moving along through the years towards a peak, both in troops deployed and in casualties. And then from that peak (1968-69 in Vietnam, 2010-11 in Afghanistan) there was a de-escalation; that is, a disengagement from casualty-incurring offensive operations that was concurrent with a withdrawal of troops.

Iraq followed a different pattern. In Iraq, we started off with the biggest numbers we could reasonably muster. There was a slight drop after that, but after that slight drop a large number of troops was maintained for several consecutive years. From 2004 till 2009, Iraq hosted anywhere between 140,000 to 170,000 American Soldiers, Sailors, Airmen, and Marines. The troop strengths tailed off starting in 2010 until the complete pullout at the end of 2011.

Afghanistan resembles the Pacific theater of World War II in that the overall Global War on Terror began with an attack on American soil planned from Afghanistan just as America's World War II began in the Pacific with an attack on American soil planned from Japan. A further similarity is that the focus of the military's efforts then shifted. A larger number of troops were committed to a different theater, which also concluded earlier. Europe and Iraq began later and ended earlier than the Pacific and Afghanistan, respectively. However, focus returned to the original theater once the second theater was concluded. The starts and finishes of the two wars went in the chiastic chronological order of A, B, B, A.

A glaring difference between the 20th and 21st century wars is the outcome of each. World War II was concluded in complete victory, both in Europe and the Pacific. Well, we don't exactly have that in these two major fronts of the GWOT; in fact, we have the exact opposite in Afghanistan.

All together, over 1,500,000 American troops served in Iraq and nearly 800,000 in Afghanistan. If it seems strange that the two decades of Afghan involvement resulted in only about half the number who served in Iraq, just remember that "the 'Stan" never had nearly as many troops committed at any given time. Only in the four years from 2009 to 2012 was US strength at over 50,000. Even at the peak in 2010-11 there were only just less than 100,000 Americans deployed.

The casualty rates, however, were similar, and this is seen in the numbers. Afghanistan had about half the number of total troops deployed as Iraq, and very roughly around half the casualties. According to the U.S. Department of Defense, Operation Iraqi Freedom (OIF) resulted in 4,431 US deaths and 31,994 wounded; the Afghan Operation Enduring Freedom (OEF) figures are 2,352 dead and 20,149 wounded.

The follow-up operations to OIF and OEF were New Dawn, Inherent Resolve, and Freedom's Sentinel. Together they resulted in 291 US deaths and 1,180 wounded.

Together with the 2,977 killed in the attacks of 2001/09/11, that amounts to 10,051 people who lost their lives to Jihadism, either on American soil or in the service of the United States.

Never Forget.

Let's turn now to the Afghan front.

Afghanistan is a landlocked country in central Asia. It's about the size of Texas with a population of about 40 million. It is linguistically and ethnically heterogenous. We will not delve into the country's fascinating anthropology here. One book I recommend to start with if you wish to investigate that angle is *Afghanistan 101: Understanding Afghan Culture* by Ehsan M. Entezar.

The following is a simple summary of the Afghan War up till the end of Operation Enduring Freedom in 2014, and it does a great job of succinctly relating the key points of each period of the conflict. It's taken from the captions to the interactive maps titled "Vicious Cycle of Afghanistan," created by Bill Roggio on the excellent site, *FDD's Long War Journal*:

Pre-9/11 | 2000

The Taliban controls nearly the entirety of 32 of Afghanistan's 34 provinces. Only Panjshir and Badakhshan, as well as small areas of neighboring provinces are controlled by the Northern Alliance.

Post-U.S. Invasion | Early 2002

The Taliban is driven from power by the U.S. with the help of the Northern Alliance and other militias. The Taliban lose control of all provincial capitals, but maintain varying degrees of presence in the provinces.

Pre-Surge | Early 2009

The Taliban reinitiated its bid to retake the country from its safe havens in Pakistan and its influence expanded in the south, east, and north. Several provincial capitals were under Taliban threat.

Post-U.S. Troop Surge | 2012

The 'Surge' was successful in relieving the pressure on the provincial capitals and driving the Taliban from key areas in the south, east, and north. The Obama Administration was clear that the increased U.S. presence would be limited to two years. The Taliban went underground and waited for U.S. forces to leave.

By 2014, the U.S. military turned over security to the Afghan military. The Taliban began to move back into traditional strongholds and take the fight to the Afghan military.

VETERANS LIVES MATTER

Ah yes, then it all came crashing down.

One does not have to be an expert in military strategy to appreciate how messed up the whole Afghan withdrawal of 2021 was. It is easily perceptible to the normal person on the street who has no military experience.

It's not my lane to decide what national policy is, nor is it that of a soldier, nor is it that of an ordinary citizen. We hire people to do that, through our electoral process. The idea is that you vet those who put their names forward to be considered for positions of public authority, and then vote on them. Theoretically, this means that enough people have trust in the winners of elections to delegate great powers to them.

We may not be involved in the fine details, but we have oversight. And so, regular folks like us should be able to clearly understand the ramifications of major affairs such as war and peace, even if we are not privy to many intricacies.

From my perspective on the ground level, as a guy on the street, I can see that the pullout as it was actually conducted from the top was just plain wrong. There are no two ways about it. I do not believe that there is any secret knowledge that the President was tapped into that would change my opinion. If he does, he has a moral duty to present it to the citizenry of the nation.

Many veterans agree that we needed to turn the country over fully to the Afghans, but the recent pullout just does not sit right. It makes many of us question why we were there in the first place, because our multi-decade effort led to such an ignominious end that was so hasty and led to such chaos. And, because it was both foreseeable and avoidable. It was seen a mile off by people who had some type of awareness. You did not even have to be an expert to know that this was coming. We saw it happen in Vietnam in 1975. We saw it happen in Iraq in 2014 with the rise of the Islamic State.

There are a lot of things that the United States cannot do, things that we do not possess the capability to accomplish. And there are things we probably ethically shouldn't do even if we did have the ability to accomplish them.

For instance, in the matter of nation building, we are not able to impose a Western culture onto a tribal culture. It is beyond us. And even if we could, should we? I, for one, would be strongly against that. Such a notion smacks of colonialism, and the American ethos has traditionally been anti-colonialist (despite the accusations I've heard personally from European socialists).

But something well within our capabilities was to foresee this disaster, and avoid it. There is no reason we could not have seen this happening in 2021. We have the clear examples from historical precedent. This is not uncharted territory. In fact, the rapid advance of an enemy in the shadow of an American pullout is becoming a recurring theme: 1975, 2014, and now in 2021.

I am absolutely not advocating for us to shoulder the entire burden of every global threat and become the world's policeman. We're not talking about that. We're talking about giving reasonable aid to people who depend on our help, and not setting our allies up for failure. To do otherwise would amount to sabotage of their efforts and their blood, as well as our American efforts and our American blood.

For civilians to tell current or former military, "Thank you for your service," is wonderful. But there is the practical aspect of honoring the collective sacrifice of the hundreds of thousands who served in Iraq, Afghanistan, and in other little hotspots around the world over the past two decades. As a bare minimum, we must respect whatever "modicum of success" has been built in whatever place our brave warriors served by *not dismantling it*.

VLM. Veterans Lives Matter.

HONOR, AND "DEPRAVED INDIFFERENCE"

For the sake of the *American* nation, we provided the hard-fought benefits of security to Afghanistan. We guaranteed our support to those who placed their full trust in us, the United States. We had given the Afghan people our full commitment.

This does *not* mean we needed to keep a permanent fighting force or pour funds into a bottomless money pit. But it does mean we needed to have the Afghans' back, to cover their "six." We needed to continue helping them for our own national security, but we also needed to stick by their side as a matter of simple honor. But we didn't.

It was simple honor itself that motivated my own military service. It motivates the service of so many of the comrades and colleagues who I served with. It's something that my buddies and I keep in our hearts. And it's something that I'd like to think is a national value that the country as a whole also keeps in mind as we deal with others around the world. As a general rule, we need to stick by our allies for the long term. It's the only honorable thing to do.

Lest we get too distracted, let's remember that the US did not abandon only Afghanistan. Our NATO and other allies involved in the Afghan project – France, Britain, Germany, among others – we also left all of them in the lurch.

It would be good to keep in mind the term "depraved indifference," which is a term used to describe the most severe form of criminal negligence. It goes beyond simple mistakes or carelessness. According to *USLegal.com*:

> "To constitute depraved indifference, the defendant's conduct must be 'so wanton, so deficient in a moral sense of concern, so lacking in regard for the life or lives of others, and so blameworthy as to warrant the same criminal liability as that which the law imposes upon a person who intentionally causes a crime."

Let's take a look at what the US leadership did. They:

1) Removed assets from Afghan forces (air, intel, logistical, etc.) which we had trained them to depend on for fighting – and then blamed the Afghans for not fighting!

Teach a man to fish, then take away his rod and blame him for not catching fish.

"It was all going to fall apart anyways." This is quite possibly a true statement. That doesn't mean we needed to help along that process and harm our vital national interest at the same time, any more than we should have helped along the collapse of the Twin Towers.

The plain fact is that the US set up the Afghans for failure over the past two decades. Creating a bloated military with all sorts of fine exteriors and fancy gizmos did not set up the Afghans for success any more than parents who spoil a child with expensive gifts to compensate for their lack of a substantive emotional relationship.

The idea was to give the Afghans the best possible chance to stand on their own two feet. But, we trained them to fight in a high-maintenance Western manner. Then at the last moment, pulled away their ability to fight in a Western manner.

For instance, we fostered their heavy dependence on technology that only we could maintain, and on air power that only we could provide. And then, at the last moment and without a proper passing of the baton, so to speak, we pulled away the contractors who operated the technology and all American air support!

How exactly was the Afghan military supposed to fight on in such circumstances? What human being, even the bravest, would so recklessly give their lives under such severe demoralization?

The Afghans needed to take responsibility for their own defense. Everyone knows that. But my point is that it's unethical for us to deny them that way of defense that we trained them up on. Two decades of close cooperation lead to a lot of symbiotic relationships that are not easily severed without severe loss of blood.

Retired British Colonel Richard Kemp related on Mark Levin's Fox show, "Life, Liberty, & Levin":

> "The reason that the Afghan National Security Forces collapsed is because he [*President Biden*] pulled the rug out from under their feet. They were doing most of the fighting in Afghanistan – not the U.S. Army, not the British Army, not the German Army. It was the Afghan Army that was doing most of the fighting, and dying in Afghanistan.
>
> But they depended heavily on air support from the United States, they depended on technical support to keep their aircraft flying, logistic support as well. And without that, they were far less capable of combat than with it."

Afghanistan is a beautiful country with enough untapped mineral resources to eventually be wealthy. But it was not yet at the point that it could have sustained that on its own.

And it was not that much for us to just provide that little bit of assistance in the background, without us engaging in combat operations, to give them that confidence. But instead, we ripped that away from them. We ripped away the technological and logistical support we had been providing them. We ripped away their air capabilities, both to strike the enemy and to evacuate casualties.

The Afghan National Army (ANA) was certainly a mixed bag in terms of quality. From what I've observed, there were a great many that were just wasting oxygen. On the other hand, there were some superb fighters as well. There were and are many Afghans who care deeply about their country.

Let's not forget that tens of thousands have been *killed* defending it over the past two decades. And this fact becomes all the more apparent if we focus on the last seven years or so since US forces ceased active combat operations. The Afghans did in fact shoulder the overwhelming majority of the brunt of their nation's defense, especially the ground combat.

2) Abandoned Bagram Airfield (the only strategic air base in the country) with great combat speed and

efficiency, and without coordinating with the Afghan relief.

Bagram Airfield was the impenetrable citadel of the NATO effort in Afghanistan. It was the nerve center from which aircraft flew out and flew in, whether to bomb the enemy, transport troops, evacuate casualties, deliver and receive supplies, or whatever else the war effort called for.

The US-led forces had uncontested control of the skies along with all the benefits that came with that. One of the primary benefits was that we could support the Afghans in their fight and Taliban & Co. could not touch us.

The base is located about an hour's drive north of the capital city of Kabul in a Dari-speaking, ethnically Tajik district. In other words, friendly territory.

It is positively dumbfounding that we would abandon one of our greatest regional assets – a fortress of strength, an oasis of hope, and a bulwark against Communist China. And we did it in a most inexplicably careless manner.

According to a World Tribune article dated 22 August, "Afghan military officials said Team Biden left by shutting off the electricity and slipping away in the night without notifying the base's new Afghan Commander, who discovered the Americans' departure more than two hours after they left."

3) Voluntarily gave up – yes, *surrendered* – the capital city of Kabul to the Taliban, even when the enemy had offered not to contest American control.

This one probably threw me for a loop the most. The reason is that I was telling everyone who had ears to listen that all we needed to do to provide a safer buffer zone and lessen the chaos was to push out from the airport and take back territory, if not the whole city of Kabul, at the least.

I was venting in August to my Afghan friend Hekmat, nicknamed "HK," about how messed up the situation was, "We have the strength to push the Taliban out of Kabul. Why doesn't the President just order an offensive to clear out the city, at the very least??"

Hekmat was heroically working to get his wife out of there. She had been patiently waiting to go through the proper administrative procedures when the Taliban's lightning offensive left her stuck behind enemy lines.

"HK, you know better than anybody, the Taliban are 'strong' against people who cannot defend themselves. I never feared them, I would go over in an instant, why the hell do we not secure a wider perimeter to let your wife and the thousands like her evacuate in safety??"

Imagine… just imagine the horror when the news broke publicly on 30 August that the Taliban had *offered* not to contest US control of Kabul until the evacuation was complete, and the US *turned them down*. How is it possible that the US leadership was determined to lose in an even more humiliating manner than our enemies - who hate us - could dream up themselves?

A lot of innocent blood is on the hands of the government/military establishment.

There were many things we could not do in Afghanistan. For instance, we could not metamorphosize the population of Afghanistan into western clones. Not that there was any attempt to impose a foreign culture *per se*, but we imported an American understanding of politics and social relations and never properly understood the local societies that composed the fabric of the country.

One thing we could still have done, at a minimum, is keep the Taliban at bay long enough to allow us to secure our own – including those Afghans who fought side by side with us, bled with us, and invested their entire lives and their entire families' lives in our promise. That was something that was within our capability and we just turned our backs on it.

The United States military has always been able to beat the Taliban on the battlefield very successfully. Unfortunately, such success does not automatically equate to winning the whole war, as this war has shown and other recent wars have also shown. But we could have at least prevented the shameful humiliation that did take place.

4) Gave the Taliban the names of American civilians in the country and of Afghans who supported us.

Delivering intelligence to the enemy is a violation of the constitutional injunction against giving them aid and comfort. It is thus one way of committing the greatest crime that one can ever commit against one's own country – treason.

The justification? Oh, we were just giving the Taliban names so we could get them through the checkpoints and into the airport.

Except, they are a terrorist enemy, we are still at war, and we would not have been put in this disgraceful position without the previous disgrace of surrendering the capital city to the enemy.

5) Refused to allow US troops to leave the confines of Kabul Airport to conduct rescues.

A – Americans and Afghan friends were thus left to make it to the airport on their own, and at the mercy of the Taliban.

The Americans, Afghans, and other who made it to the airport on their own had to go through Taliban checkpoints where many of them were beaten. Some were killed, and I know this on good authority.

I never bought into the bizarre anti-French bias that bubbled around in the US in the few years following the 9/11 terror attacks. Who could really argue against things named for freedom, but French fries had a fine name already.

As Americans, we really have no cause to have any such sentiments about France. Not only is she our oldest and historically most consistent ally, but she has provided tremendous help in the GWOT. Beyond that, Uncle Sam would have a tough time looking Marianne in the eyes to make fun of her for surrendering to the Nazis who overpowered France with a violent *Blitzkrieg*. Under President Biden's direct orders, the US ran away cowering before a rag-tag bunch of Third World Jihadists.

And in any case, French troops left the confines of the airport to rescue hundreds of their citizens while American troops were being forced by their leaders to stay behind barricades. SecDef Austin's excuse was that US forces did not have the capability to retrieve large numbers of people.

The credibility of such an assertion can hardly stand, because the French, the British, and other nations actually went out into Kabul and aggressively rescued the stranded. Are we to believe that they had some advanced capabilities that America did not?

B – Thousands of US and allied troops were jam packed into a relatively small area to be sitting ducks for attacks.

Even civilian friends of mine asked me what the sense was of having all those Soldiers and other servicemembers filling up that airport, close together, and bunched up to be targets for the enemy. A "mission of mercy" was fine as long as our guys were prepared for war, because we were at war. Even President Biden acknowledged that it did not end until 30 August. But our guys were set up at the airport at a great disadvantage before the enemy. The Taliban dominated everything outside of the airport, so there was no way to properly execute the "mission of mercy" the President called for.

C – When troops and civilians were inevitably killed, the US leadership retaliated with a deliberate precision strike that did not kill a single terrorist, but did kill several little children.

While we cannot force a rebuilt nation onto the population of Afghanistan, we certainly possess the capability to secure an area of territory and allow for a robust evacuation plan to be executed. And the murder of those gallant 13 servicemembers, mostly Marines – this too was predictable. It did not have to be like this.

6) Ignored the counsel of allies in order to rush out of the country according to the timeline the Taliban ordered the US to follow.

The deadline of 31 August was initially decided upon by President Biden. However, it soon became an opportunity for the Taliban to flex their newfound authority. These tough guys had the nerve to tell us we had to leave by that date or there would consequences. We should have stayed longer just for this alone!

The deadline was too soon, and the President gave no leeway. He forced our allies to comply with a deadline they were not ready for. And he violated his word to stay until all citizens were out. The creation and enforcement of this deadline is an example of incompetent leadership, to put it mildly. It is perhaps **the single factor most responsible** for the chaotic results. Of all the highly knowledgeable military folks I spoke to on this issue, there was not a single one who thought the inflexibility of the deadline was a good idea.

7) Gave the Taliban unprecedented leverage over the US and others through negligent abandonment of:

A - American citizens

The values of the American combat soldier are encoded in the creeds he recites. All Army infantrymen will be familiar with the Ranger Creed, which expresses the core values that spur him to accept mortal danger:

> "I will never leave a fallen comrade to fall into the hands of the enemy and under no circumstances will I ever embarrass my country.
>
> Readily will I display the intestinal fortitude required to fight on to the Ranger objective and complete the mission though I be the lone survivor."

Just imagine the level of depraved indifference required to allow terrified American citizens and allies fleeing for their lives to fend for themselves in the midst of sadistic terrorists. Imagine our servicemembers having no control over missions that violated their consciences. Many of our guys are suffering trauma from this, and understandably so.

The only thing I can connect the feeling to is stories I've heard from those who had been sexually abused by figures of authority close to them. The descriptions are shockingly similar to the feelings that so many combat veterans describe when talking about the Afghan withdrawal. *When those you trust violate the very principles you have given your life to, and at the real risk of losing your* literal *life in the case of the military, it is a spear through the heart.*

B - Afghan allies

The abandonment of the Afghan people is a human issue, transcending political ideologies.

It is a real-life matter concerning people who invested their lives and everything they have and own to stand by us. They stood by the United States and they stood by their own country – they did good by their own nation

THE GREAT SABOTAGE

in their own eyes. They saw the partnership with the US as something that could be trusted.

One group of Afghans I wish to single out because of their loyal and essential battlefield service is our interpreters, affectionately known as "terps." One man who knows better than most about the work of our terps is Bryn Reynolds, who was my boss downrange and also the best Platoon Sergeant I ever had in my military career. In an interview with Trishna Begam of ABC News 10, Albany, NY, he gives a superb and succinct description of their value:

> We did make a huge commitment to a lot of the people that risked their lives to help us during the last 20 years. And I'm speaking specifically, because that's who I worked with the most, were the interpreters. Um, I had two that were embedded with me that there's *no way* I could have done the work that I did without them. And a lot of people don't realize that for a combat unit, those guys are not just interpreters where they're [*only*] interpreting the language for you.
>
> They're fighters, they're well-seasoned fighters. They are your cultural liaisons, and they will help you navigate some of the different intricacies of

different villages. You know, from one mountain range to the other, you might be dealing with Pashto and then Dari [*the two main languages of the country*] and they have different sets of norms and culture over there. They help you navigate that. They help you barter in the market if you have to buy some food for your soldiers.

They do everything for you. And we were very lucky that the interpreters that we fell in on that were embedded with us had multiple years, multiple army units rotate through them. They had a lot of experience and they were our guides.

And then we hear about the terp who guided then-Senator Biden around the country begging the now-President to save his life.

The term "depraved indifference" come to mind as an accurate descriptor.

C - contract work dogs and rescue dogs

This is an issue close to my heart because I am dog guy, and was a professional Explosive Detection Canine Handler, and the cause to have my retirement age partner returned to me has gained a large measure of popular support (look up "Bring K9 Mattie Home).

I am afraid that the military gave a false impression concerning the dogs that were abandoned at the Hamid Karzai International Airport.

It was claimed that no *military* dogs were left behind, and this is true. But the US military had the responsibility for everybody's security, and a great many contract working dogs were abandoned. I have confirmed with sources I know close to the events that this is the case.

The Afghan withdrawal is a human tragedy, but we have swept up these innocent creatures in its wake as well. Our loyal canine partners deserve far better than being left to fend for themselves in the streets and abandoned tarmacs.

D - many billions of dollars worth of lethal and "sensitive item" arms and equipment

Gen. McKenzie has made the point that much of the abandoned equipment was rendered useless before the US departed. But why did perfectly good military items have to be destroyed in the first place? Perhaps that's what you have to do if you're Norway getting overrun by the Nazi Germany, or Hungary getting overrun by Soviet Russia.

But this is the United States of America fleeing before the Tali.. *who?*

The point cannot be stressed enough that it was easily within the power of our forces to keep the bad guys at bay. And, it would have been worth it to do so even for the equipment alone.

Many American items cost an astronomical sum. The money to pay for that is not created by the government, which is not a wealth creating entity. It is taken from American workers.

For instance, I've spent many hours riding around some dangerous territory in a Mine-Resistant Ambush Protected (MRAP) armored vehicle. I don't think I'd be able to buy one though – each individual one costs from half a million to one million dollars, depending on the model and the accessories. Not many of us can pull that kind of cash out of our pockets. And yet, we actually did pay for the wantonly abandoned items with money out of our pockets.

Certainly, a government has a right to collect taxes, within limits. But every dollar represents someone's sweat. Needlessly destroying the world's finest equipment is a profound disrespect to the American worker.

Thoughtlessly casting away the dear products of our nation's labor when there was no true military need to do so is just plain *mindboggling*.

But its even worse than this. One cop-out I've heard is that much of the equipment wasn't really ours, it was that of the Afghan forces. We had given it to them through the years in order to outfit them with the best stuff to fight the Jihadists. Well, one would hope that this stuff would be working. And much of it was.

And now, it's all in the hands of the Taliban. The Jihadist group is now perhaps the best outfitted terrorist organization in the world, courtesy of the sweat, tears, and yes, *blood* of American labor. I don't have statistics on it, but my anecdotal impression is that the average patriotic American worker is not pleased with this situation, to put it mildly.

And wait yes, it's *even worse* than this, yet again.

The most advanced items of this equipment are being sent to Communist China to be reverse engineered.

Dear LORD, help us.

THE RIGHT WAY TO HAVE WITHDRAWN

Was there really no better way?

There was a decent, dutiful soldier who I was conversing with about the disaster. While he was as upset about it as you would expect, he also said, "I am a just a junior servicemember, so I don't Monday morning quarterback my seniors."

Sigh.

In normal circumstances, this is precisely the attitude to have. You cannot have a functioning military with overt disorder in the ranks. Discipline must be maintained and authority must be respected. Such respect for authority is both a means and an end. As an end, a functioning hierarchy of some sort is simply the natural order in any organized grouping of humans. As a means, the hierarchy is geared towards the accomplishment of a greater end for the good of all.

The underlying assumption is that the leadership of an institution is working for this common good. This is not to say they wouldn't have personal motivations as well, we all do. But they put the organization first, because the organization is a notional stand-in for the individuals who compose it. When one speaks of "the Constitution" it's really not the piece of paper that matters for its own sake, but rather the people of the nation whose rights it legally guarantees.

Alas, these are not normal circumstances. They are abnormal, in the extreme.

Throwing a game is considered the gravest kind of scandal in the sports world. Those who hold positions of trust in the American military structure forfeit any credibility if they *throw a war*.

So let's do some Monday morning quarterbacking. It's entirely warranted in the circumstances, and it's really not too complicated here.

Well now, how could it have been done better, and with a relative ease that calls into play the numerous strengths of the American military?

If we had already been reduced to the Kabul airport enclave, we would have *at a minimum* had to establish a secure perimeter *outside* of the airport, to allow for a buffer zone through which we could then filter and vet civilians. The more territory under our control, the better. The perimeter would be several layers deep and consist of both hard defenses that would include gates and checkpoints, as well as a more mobile screening force. We would then slowly, carefully, and on our own timeline evacuate civilians. And dogs. All American and allied equipment would then be sent away.

Finally, we would pull back the screening forces. The military are the last people out. The final act would be to destroy the base/airport so as not to let it be usable to the enemy. This is all obvious.

Well, it was either not obvious to the guys in charge, or was obvious and ignored.

Some of this is so common sense that a hilarious meme was circulating which depicted a parody of the "For Dummies" book series. The image title says "Leaving Afghanistan For Dummies" with the trademark yellow background, under which was "EASY Checklist! – Civilians first – Equipment next – Soldiers last – Destroy base."

If we are imagining that we have more than just Kabul, or had started earlier with serious plans for a **robust withdrawal in strength that would have protected our friends and fended off the Taliban**, far more possibilities open up.

You *always* cover your withdrawal by some means, even if you are otherwise in an untenable position.

THE GREAT SABOTAGE

The following passage is from the memoir of America's great chaplain of World War I, Father Francis Duffy. He describes the Fighting 69th being stopped in front of the German wire at the *Kriemhilde Stellung* during the Meuse-Argonne campaign in October, 1918. Wild Bill Donovan's leadership on that day earned him the Medal of Honor. He knew to **cover the American withdrawal**:

> *"By 11:00 o'clock Donovan had decided that the 1st Battalion had too many losses to make it possible for them to get through. He told Anderson, who was with him, to return and bring forward his battalion so that Kelly's men and their wounded could pass through... This relief was begun about noon with the aid of a heavy barrage from our artillery."*

The guiding principle of protecting what is vulnerable from exterior threat with a barrier of separation is intrinsic to the natural order, and we see it play out in our everyday existence. This is why skin covers our vital organs; our vital organs do not lie outside of our skin.

SEEING IT COMING

Nearly all of it really was predictable. I mentioned on national television (CNN's *New Day*, 17 August 2021) that distinguished military experts such as GEN. (Ret) Jack

Keane and MAJ (Ret) Donald Vandergriff had already sounded the clarion call. And in fact, I was recently looking over some notes I took in recent years and refreshed my memory that I had said precisely the same thing before, if only in private notes to myself.

It's not that I have any special powers of foresight, but those that have even a modicum of basic military wisdom, and even people on the street, can see that executing a withdrawal from a war zone has to be done in a manner that protects your friends. And, you don't throw away the entirety of whatever "modicum of success" was accomplished, because that's **the only tangible memorial of the sacrifices** of our Soldiers, Sailors, Airmen, and Marines.

In a 2020 article in the legendary *Stars and Stripes*, commemorating the 19th anniversary of the September 11 attacks, reporter J.P. Lawrence accurately related one of my thoughts on the situation at that time:

> "Fennessy said he thinks the militants signed the Doha deal primarily to get U.S. forces out of the country before they stage an armed takeover.
>
> If that is the case, and if Afghanistan is allowed to fall apart after the U.S. leaves, the deaths on 9/11

and during America's longest war will have been in vain, he said."

Unfortunately, I was correct.

The reality was even worse than my original concern. The thing I could not imagine at the time was that Afghanistan would be allowed to fall *before* the US left. This has simply *never* happened at the conclusion a major war in all of American history.

Even Barack Obama, whose total withdrawal from Iraq allowed for rise of the sadistic Islamic State of Iraq and Syria (ISIS), had enough sense to send a force back in to pull the region back from the brink. Perhaps he didn't want to be known as a President who lost the first American war since Vietnam; whatever his personal motivation, he did the right thing in this circumstance. His successor finished the job, and Iraq still stands as of this writing.

The following is my interview with J.P. Lawrence, conducted online, from March of 2020 (the original article was never printed because the COVID pandemic interrupted operations; a modified version came out in September of that year, as referenced earlier). I had first met the reporter years earlier when he was a student at

Columbia University and some of my work had caught his attention.

Since the interview captured my take on the situation before any of the tragedy of 2021 took place, it is enlightening:

> J.P. - When were you in Afghanistan last? I remember you used to bagpipe there.
>
> SÉAMUS - Me? No, I was never a bagpiper. A singer though, particularly Irish tunes. I should say I *am* a singer lol. Exactly 10 years ago to the week I landed in country. So it's pretty ironic we're in touch right now, this is a significant anniversary for me.
>
> J.P. - Wow, yeah.
>
> SÉAMUS - March-Dec 2010, the biggest year of the war for us, when the US had both the most troops deployed and the most killed of any year, 500 (499 to be exact)
>
> J.P. - Where were you sent?
>
> SÉAMUS - Throughout RC [*Regional Command*] East - primarily COP [*Combat Outpost*] Band-e Sardeh in Andar District of Ghazni Province, FOB

[*Forward Operating Base*] Lightning, and FOB Red Hill.

J.P. - Oh s**t, yeah that area is some rough s**t. Especially Ghanzi right now. How are you feeling on the ten-year anniversary?

SÉAMUS - Mixed feelings about a variety of aspects of it. But on a personal level, I've been hit with a certain nostalgia or at least affection for the time I served there - the brotherhood forged in battle, the life and death nature of it all, the beautiful country of Afghanistan.

Ghazni was rough s**t 10 years ago. I remember wondering as a kid how Vietnam veterans felt knowing that the country they fought to save from Communism eventually fell to the enemy. I was a little curious how polls showed that the vast majority were immensely proud and would do it again, even in such circumstances. I get it now. I would have loved if we had swooped in and permanently wiped out the Taliban in the area. We could come back years later and visit with our children like some WWI & II vets did in Europe. That was not to be the case. But even with the bad guys now running amok in the very areas that we fought them - and defeated them - **I would do it again**. I am proud of having lived and fought side by side with my brothers in arms. I am proud of our tactical victories against some crazy odds. And if Andar district was eventually lost, I know that it was not us who lost it. **We did our jobs** exactly like we came to do.

J.P.: The deal, the details about the Taliban entering powersharing, how does that affect your understanding of the sacrifices you and others made?

SÉAMUS: I have a personal interest in following how things play out over the upcoming years, even decades, precisely because of the sacrifices we made. 2,309 Americans killed. 20,660 wounded, many of them maimed [*stats as I had them in early 2020*]. **It better have been worth it**.

Of course it is widely recognized that the previous situation of a perpetual war was untenable. But vigilance by our country in ensuring that jihadists no longer have power in Afghanistan is a requirement. Not necessarily a renewed and certainly not a permanent troop commitment, but vigilance, and decisive action if necessary.

It really infuriated me when ISIS overran much of Iraq, because the insurgent cause from which they were born had already been defeated. Thankfully the President [*Trump*] was decisive in suppressing the Islamic State, but not until a lot of blood had been spilled. It did not have to erupt that way in the first place had we been vigilant in maintaining the peace.

The worrisome part is that American policy changes when administrations change, leaving the sacrifices of our servicemembers at the mercy of people with differing foreign and defense attitudes and policies.

In Vietnam, a similar peace deal was made. And we promised to have South Vietnam's back if the North were to do anything again. The US administration changed, the North invaded, and Vietnam was lost.

We can prevent a similar thing from happening again. But history worries me, as does **the fickleness of US political cycles.**

This is a matter of profound significance, because no matter what the Taliban actually say, they cannot be trusted. Every indication is they are just agreeing to terms to get our forces out of the country so they caṇ have a free hand to take over again. Maybe not immediately, but when they think the American public has forgotten or won't care. If our country does get collectively lazy in remembering those who fought and served where I was 10 years ago and where you are now at the moment, it would be **spitting in the face of all of us**. In a nutshell.

This was prescient. The above was true even in normal circumstances. But the wild card I was not quite expecting, the "X factor" that allowed the Jihadist enemies of the United States to achieve the most stunning victory ever won against the United States, was the President himself, Joseph R. Biden. It is now clear after the September 28, 2021, testimony of top Pentagon officials on Capitol Hill that the orders which caused the catastrophe really did come from the top.

This is why my conscience compels me to speak about the President in relation to the Afghan disaster. Initially, I was hesitant. Having had spent years as a professional soldier, publicly airing personal opinions about the top boss had never been a thing of mine. Also, I did not wish to let frustration make me lay blame in the wrong direction. Nobody likes being falsely accused; in fact, God Himself doesn't like it which is why the injunction against bearing false witness is a commandment.

But as the truth emerged, it became clear that the man most responsible for everything that went wrong with the pullout – and not just indirectly through delegation but through the direct exercise of his authority – was President Biden himself.

And he did so in a manner which establishes probable cause that he broke the supreme Law of the Land, the very same supreme law he is mandated under oath to be the chief defender of, and which everyone who serves under him is also under oath to support and defend.

This is why he cannot be left off the hook; as we speak about in Section IV, he must be held accountable. An honest assessment will lead an honest person to this non-partisan conclusion. His misdirection was so egregious that anyone of sound mind who defends it, or who argues for a punishment less than the full justice allowed by the Constitution, must be suspected of doing so for partisan reasons.

J.P.: I've been talking to some gold star families right now, how they make sense of it all.

They grieve, but they tell me their loved ones died fighting for something they believe in.

But how does that work now? If the Taliban aren't going to be defeated.

SÉAMUS: Like I was saying above, it's the knowledge that the soldier in question, alive or dead, did their job - **they won the battle on the ground**, as they trained to do. **There is comfort in that.**

There is simultaneously a sense of bitterness against the politicians and bureaucrats for **big picture incompetence**. It is easy to blame them, and probably appropriate too.

The fighting man on the ground, and his family, can thus view the war with a **clean conscience**, knowing they did their part.

I stand by these words as much now as I ever have.

Politicians and bureaucrats (including military bureaucrats) are indeed easy targets. But shall we consider that perhaps we are going too harsh on them? Would we do any different if we were in their shoes?

In the practical sphere, such questions are moot because these people are actually the ones who have the power. They chose these fields of endeavor in life, and it is only right that they fully shoulder the burden of responsibility that comes along with them.

We have been dishonored by our highest leaders, and they must be held accountable.

I. HELPFUL ARTICLES

Blitzer, Ronn. "Taliban offered Kabul to U.S. but Americans said no: report." *Fox News*, August 30, 2021.

Brufke, Juliegrace. "Fleeing Americans beaten by Taliban in Kabul, Pentagon chief tells Congress." *New York Post*, August 20, 2021.

Davis, Jack. "US troops blitz outside of airport walls; brief expedition brings 169 American citizens into airport." *Western Journal*, August 22, 2021.

Gartner, Scott S. "Iraq and Afghanistan through the lens of American military casualties." *Small Wars Journal*, April 3, 2013.

"Here's why August 31 is deadline for US pullout from Afghanistan as Taliban warn against extension." (AFP). *News 18*, August 25, 2021.

"Kabul blast: US responsible for airport security, say Taliban, condemn blasts." (Team Hindu). *Hindustan Times*, August 26, 2021.

"Kash Patel: Trump would never have given up Bagram Air Base." (World Tribune Staff). *World Tribune*, August 22, 2021.

Keller, Jared. "Here's all the US military equipment that likely ended up in Taliban hands." *Task and Purpose*, August 18, 2021.

Schogol, Jeff. "'Modicum of Success' is the new 'Mission Accomplished' for Afghanistan." *Task and Purpose*, December 5, 2020.

Seligman, Lara, Alexander Ward, and Andrew Desiderio. "U.S. officials provided Taliban with names of Americans, Afghan allies to evacuate." *Politico*, August 26, 2021.

Steinbuch, Yaron. "American Humane group says US left military dogs behind in Afghanistan." *New York Post*, August 31, 2021.

Trevithick, Joseph. "Kabul Airport's abandoned dogs are now on the loose and the Taliban want to round them up." *The War Zone*, September 1, 2021.

Webb, James. "As US military sticks to airport, British and French forces are rescuing their citizens in Kabul: reports." *Military Times*, August 19, 2021.

II. THE ESTABLISHMENT'S RESPONSE

This section will analyze the slick verbal maneuvering used by the leadership of the US government to rationalize the preventable disaster of the Afghan pullout. The result of this official oratory was the creation of a false alternative narrative in conjunction with the simultaneous obfuscation of the real issues.

The centerpiece of the analysis is the speech given at the conclusion of the US withdrawal by the Commander in Chief. It is called "Remarks by President Biden on the End of the War in Afghanistan" and was delivered from the White House's State Dining Room in the mid-afternoon of August 31, 2021.

Washington Post columnist James Hohmann said immediately following its delivery that his impression was that it was "the strongest speech he's given yet" on the issue of the withdrawal from Afghanistan. Having seen many of President Biden's speeches and interviews on the subject, I agree with Hohmann's assessment.

THE ESTABLISHMENT'S RESPONSE

As such, it makes a perfect specimen of the establishment's rhetoric to dissect. No excuse can be made that it was some series of off-the-cuff remarks that should not be taken seriously. It was carefully written and constructed to put the Biden Administration's best arguments forward.

Reference will also be made to some of his other comments, as well as to the public statements of Secretary of Defense Lloyd Austin and Chairman of the Joint Chiefs of Staff General Mark A. Milley.

In much of my commentary, I speak in the second person, as if I am actually addressing those to whom I am responding.

This transcript is directly from WhiteHouse.gov (oratorical flubs are included, as in the original; words with lines through them are what was actually said, and the adjacent words in brackets are what was supposed to have been said):

> Last night in Kabul, the United States ended 20 years of war in Afghanistan — the longest war in American history.

President Biden is declaring 30 August 2021 to be the end date of the Afghan War. We will come back to this.

> *We completed one of the biggest airlifts in history, with more than 120,000 people evacuated to safety. That number is more than double what most experts thought were possible. No nation — no nation has ever done anything like it in all of history. Only the United States had the capacity and the will and the ability to do it, and we did it today.*
>
> *The extraordinary success of this mission was due to the incredible skill, bravery, and selfless courage of the United States military and our diplomats and intelligence professionals.*

I wholeheartedly agree with this praise of our gallant heroes and the capabilities of our great nation.

Let's not forget the source of the manufactured rush out of the country. This seems to me akin to an inebriated vehicle operator who rams into another car. He praises the EMS who rush to rescue the innocent victims, but without any of the remorse that one would expect even from a drunk driver.

> *For weeks, they risked their lives to get American citizens, Afghans who helped us, citizens of our Allies and partners, and others onboard planes and out of the country. And they did it facing a crush of*

enormous crowds seeking to leave the country. And they did it knowing ISIS-K terrorists — sworn enemies of the Taliban — were lurking in the midst of those crowds.

ISIS-K is the "Islamic State – Khorasan Province," that is, the Afghan branch of this Jihadist movement. President Biden's reference to them is exceptionally slick. By emphasizing that they are the "sworn enemies of the Taliban," he is setting up the idea that they are the real bad guys, and the Taliban really aren't so bad after all.

My impression is that either the President truly believes this, in which case he is *wrong* and displays clearly impaired judgement; or, he is deliberately spinning it this way in order to lessen the culpability of his cooperation with the Taliban, in which case it is deceitful and utterly insidious.

800,000 US troops were deployed to fight the Taliban. Tens of thousands of American casualties (between killed and wounded) were suffered at their hands. The Taliban are the bad guys. Let us never be in doubt about that.

But then how, you might ask, could we negotiate the Doha Agreement of 2020 with them?

Negotiating with an enemy for your side's benefit is a historically accepted practice and is distinct in its very substance from rolling over in submission to them.

In reality, all these Jihadist groups hold to versions of the same core ideology, despite having a diversity of foci. The Taliban focuses on central Asia, while Al-Qaeda and ISIS are more internationalist. But even if they are different *from* each other and have differences *with* each other, they all *hate America*.

It's like how McDonald's, Burger King, and Wendy's are different, but they are *far* more similar to each other than any of them are to Hewlett Packard or Microsoft.

Not only is hating America and promoting their own brand of Islamist radicalism something that unites all those groups, but hating America is sufficient common ground for the Taliban to partner with atheistic Communist China.

No Mr. President, just *no*. Please don't insult our intelligence by implying ISIS-K *bad*, but Taliban *not so bad* (along with Al-Qaeda to boot, because they stand together with the Taliban).

THE ESTABLISHMENT'S RESPONSE

> *And still, the men and women of the United States military, our diplomatic corps, and intelligence professionals did their job and did it well, risking their lives not for professional gains but to serve others; not in a mission of war but in a mission of mercy.*
>
> *Twenty servicemembers were wounded in the service of this mission. Thirteen heroes gave their lives.*

This statement about the mission being one of mercy but not of war is exceptionally problematic.

The problem is not with the "mission of mercy" exactly, but that our troops were sent *into a war* without being sent on a *mission of war*. To send our troops into mortal danger without putting them on a war footing to defend their lives is gravely immoral. President Biden started his speech by saying that the war ended on 30 August, so even in his mind the war was still going on when he sent our troops in. And yet, for him it was not a mission of war.

If these heroes lost their lives fighting to take back territory, there would be less public anger over it. But in fact, they were left packed together as sitting ducks in a war zone.

This has to be criminal on some level.

I was just at Dover Air Force Base for the dignified transfer. We owe them and their families a debt of gratitude we can never repay but we should never, ever, ever forget.

The dignified transfer involved President Biden continuously looking at his watch as if in boredom.

Initially, when I heard that he looked at his watch during the offload of our servicemembers' caskets from the plane, I thought people might have been going too hard on him; it seemed like sensationalism. Anybody, even a President, should be able to check the time if needed without people getting on their case, right? But as it turns out, there was more to the story.

President Biden kept glancing at his watch as each casket was unloaded, several times, and in a manner **overtly disrespectful** to the solemnity of the occasion.

Dignified.

We do indeed owe the fallen and their families a debt of gratitude that can never be repaid and should never be forgotten. This comment is true.

THE ESTABLISHMENT'S RESPONSE

> *In April, I made the decision to end this war. As part of that decision, we set the date of August 31st for American troops to withdraw.*

Inflexible, top-down, pie-in-the-sky megalomania. This infernal artificial deadline was the very kindling of the 5-alarm fire, the primer that set off the round in the chamber, the fuse that detonated the grenade. Implicit in this comment is the idea that war is like a light switch that a President can just make a decision to flick off.

> *The assumption was that more than 300,000 Afghan National Security Forces that we had trained over the past two decades and equipped would be a strong adversary in their civil wars with the Taliban.*

> *That assumption — that the Afghan government would be able to hold on for a period of time beyond military drawdown — turned out not to be accurate.*

We already dealt with this nonsense in Section I.

It is rather brazen of the President to engineer the conditions that put the Afghan nation in the worst possible position to oppose the Taliban, but then blame them for the collapse as if he had nothing to do with it. And, the previous month, Biden seriously wanted Afghan President Ashraf Ghani to knowingly present a fake picture of success. As our President told theirs, "Things aren't going well in terms of the fight against the Taliban. And there's a need, *whether it's true or not* [emphasis added], there is a need to project a different picture." It's a revealing insight into the mind of Joe Biden.

> *But I still instructed our national security team to prepare for every eventuality — even that one. And that's what we did.*
>
> *So, we were ready when the Afghan Security Forces — after two decades of fighting for their country and losing thousands of their own — did not hold on as long as anyone expected.*

The finger pointing and blaming goes on and on...

> *We were ready when they and the people of Afghanistan watched their own government collapse and their president flee amid the corruption and malfeasance, handing over the country to their enemy, the Taliban, and significantly increasing the risk to U.S. personnel and our Allies.*

I don't know that we were ready for it, but now the people of America watched our own government facilitate the collapse of an ally, and our President sit comfortably amid the corruption and malfeasance, handing over the allied

THE ESTABLISHMENT'S RESPONSE

country to our enemy, the Taliban, and significantly increasing the risk to US personnel and our allies.

> *As a result, to safely extract American citizens before August 31st — as well as embassy personnel, Allies and partners, and those Afghans who had worked with us and fought alongside of us for 20 years — I had authorized 6,000 troops — American troops — to Kabul to help secure the airport.*

You sent more than twice as many American troops as it took to drive the Taliban from the entire country in 2001. And you placed them all into a single airport?

> *As General McKenzie said, this is the way the mission was designed. It was designed to operate under severe stress and attack. And that's what it did.*

More rhetorical flourish to spin the tale that somehow this is just exactly how we envisioned it to turn out.

You still have not addressed how you set up the "severe stress and attack" in the first place by demoralizing the Afghans and encouraging the enemy. Aside from the actions you took to leave our friends without support, your own weak personality encouraged the Taliban. They took a calculated risk that you would respond with total impotence, and they were correct.

> Since March, we reached out 19 times to Americans in Afghanistan, with multiple warnings and offers to help them leave Afghanistan — all the way back as far as March.

It really doesn't matter how many times you reached out. Phrasing it this way puts the statement perilously close to victim blaming.

> After we started the evacuation 17 days ago, we did initial outreach and analysis and identified around 5,000 Americans who had decided earlier to stay in Afghanistan but now wanted to leave.
>
> Our Operation ~~Allied Rescue~~ [Allies Refuge] ended up getting more than 5,500 Americans out. We got out thousands of citizens and diplomats from those countries that went into Afghanistan with us to get bin Laden. We got out locally employed staff of the United States Embassy and their families, totaling roughly 2,500 people. We got thousands of Afghan translators and interpreters and others, who supported the United States, out as well.

THE ESTABLISHMENT'S RESPONSE

> *Now we believe that about 100 to 200 Americans remain in Afghanistan with some intention to leave. Most of those who remain are dual citizens, long-time residents who had earlier decided to stay because of their family roots in Afghanistan.*

It's good you are lauding the accomplishments of those who did amazing things to clean up a disaster you were the catalyst for. What about those Americans left behind who were caring for immobile sick relatives, or those stuck in remote provinces? Even you admit that "most" had earlier decided to stay, which is equivalent to saying "some" did not choose to stay. And even of those who earlier decided to stay, "earlier" implies that they were probably not under Taliban rule at the time, and that they made their previous decisions according to that understanding. So what now?

Also, 100 to 200 is a rather wide range. And, it's likely there were many more. But the bigger problem is that *any* were left behind. This is **directly contrary to the values of the US military.**

The severity of the double-cross is compounded by what you told George Stephanopoulos to his face when he directly questioned you on *what if* we couldn't get every American out by 31 August: "If there's American citizens left, we're going to stay until we get them all out."

> *The bottom line: ~~Ninety~~ [Ninety-eight] percent of Americans in Afghanistan who wanted to leave were able to leave.*
>
> *And for those remaining Americans, there is no deadline. We remain committed to get them out if they want to come out. Secretary of State Blinken is leading the continued diplomatic efforts to ensure a safe passage for any American, Afghan partner, or foreign national who wants to leave Afghanistan.*

What you're saying to those Americans remaining, to that two percent, is that they were just not important enough to wait for. As a veteran who takes seriously the American military ethic of leaving *nobody* behind, this is simply repugnant – and it's coming from the boss himself.

In addition, the lack of a sense of urgency is quite disturbing. "Sure, we firefighters remain committed to getting you out of the burning building if you want to come out. As we stand here by the truck waiting for you to come out of the blazing inferno on your own. Just make it to the door yourself, we'll try to do the rest. Hurry up, our dinner is getting cold."

> *In fact, just yesterday, the United Nations Security Council passed a resolution that sent a clear message*

about what the international community expects the Taliban to deliver on moving forward, notably freedom of travel, freedom to leave. And together, we are joined by over 100 countries that are determined to make sure the Taliban upholds those commitments.

What kind of joke is this? Sending "a clear message" because the Taliban would not have misbehaved if previous messages weren't so unclear? And "the international community *expects* the Taliban to deliver." Yes, what strong language. Because everyone is "*determined* to make sure" through... resolutions?

I'm not knocking UNSC resolutions *per se*; sometimes there are things the international community agrees on and wants to put out a resolution about.

But, **if the *strongest* leverage at our disposal – military force – cannot make the Taliban comply with our desires, what leads you to believe that *lesser* means will?**

It will include ongoing efforts in Afghanistan to reopen the airport, as well as overland routes, allowing for continued departure to those who want

> to leave and delivery of humanitarian assistance to the people of Afghanistan.

A most utopian view of totalitarian rule by Taliban terrorists, and US cooperation with them. "Efforts," to reopen this stuff that you already had complete access to before you voluntarily lost it.

> The Taliban has made public commitments, broadcast on television and radio across Afghanistan, on safe passage for anyone wanting to leave, including those who worked alongside Americans. We don't take them by their word alone but by their actions, and we have leverage to make sure those commitments are met.

Public commitments of the Taliban? Leverage?

I SAY AGAIN: **If the *strongest* leverage at our disposal – military force – cannot make the Taliban comply with our desires, what leads you to believe that *lesser* means will?**

Especially if you're taking military force off the table as an option.

> Let me be clear: Leaving August the 31st is not due to an arbitrary deadline; it was designed to save American lives.

When I heard the President saying this, the words of Jesus Christ immediately came to mind: "For whoever would save his life will lose it; and whoever loses his life for my sake and the gospel's will save it." (Gospel of Mark, 8:35 RSV). And within this Gospel which the Lord tells us is worth dying for, He instructs us that "greater love has no man than this, that a man lay down his life for his friends" (Gospel of John, 15:13 RSV).

There is a world of difference between, on the one hand, saving your life through a gutless shirking of responsibility, and on the other hand, saving the lives of others as well as your own soul by behaving with honor. The difference is the difference between heaven and hell, literally.

Fleeing even before a strong enemy is unacceptable. I'm not talking about tactical retreats, wherein you temporarily cede territory in order to gain some type of an advantage. In such a case, the soldier is still fighting. No, I am talking about *fleeing*, yellow-bellied running away.

If running away before even a strong enemy is unacceptable, how much more so if we are fleeing from a force we can easily defend against?

I cannot tolerate craven cowardice. It is unbecoming in even the lowest ranking private soldier; indeed, most privates in these wars have shown exceptional bravery. Cowardice, particularly when deceitfully cloaked as courage, is that much more intolerable coming from the Commander in Chief of the Armed Forces, by many orders of magnitude.

Everything I have read suggests that the "No Later Than" date of 31 August was chosen so as not to make President Biden look bad by pulling out on the 20th anniversary of the 9/11 attacks. It would be bad optics. That's ironic, considering how bad everything ended up actually being. Bad optics indeed!

The one exception to this explanation is the Administration's own account that the date was set because the military didn't need any more time than that to evacuate everyone.

Even if that were true, it turns out that more time was needed for a complete evacuation, yet the date was adhered to as if it were more important than the people abandoned in its wake. There is still no reasonable justification given for why no flexibility was built into the date to better respond to the situation on the ground.

THE ESTABLISHMENT'S RESPONSE

> *My predecessor, the former President, signed an agreement with the Taliban to remove U.S. troops by May the 1st, just months after I was inaugurated. It included no requirement that the Taliban work out a cooperative governing arrangement with the Afghan government, but it did authorize the release of 5,000 prisoners last year, including some of the Taliban's top war commanders, among those who just took control of Afghanistan.*
>
> *And by the time I came to office, the Taliban was in its strongest military position since 2001, controlling or contesting nearly half of the country.*

The Afghan situation at the beginning of 2021 was absolutely problematic. That's why in Section 0, I said that it was a hazardous, unsteady stalemate before the withdrawal. But one does not have to be smarter than a 5th grader to understand that "controlling or contesting nearly half" of something means that over half is not controlled or contested.

Further, "contested" means the issue is not settled and either side has a fighting chance.

It's not entirely clear at this point who was ultimately at fault for the release of 5,000 prisoners. I absolutely was disturbed by it. But that is not what caused the collapse of the country.

I've been disturbed by many aspects of our involvement in the past two decades, but those deeds had already been done. It was a part of history. But the collapse of 2021 was an immediately present situation that needed to be dealt with decisively as it happened.

Well, it was dealt with decisively, by our own team captain scoring the winning goal for the opposing team. President Biden's misdirection of the American and allied withdrawal created the conditions for the Jihadist terrorists to take nearly complete control. Forget about "contested"; they massacred the pro-freedom opposition.

The Taliban certainly did "Build Back Better."

> *The previous administration's agreement said that if we stuck to the May 1st deadline that they had signed on to leave by, the Taliban wouldn't attack any American forces, but if we stayed, all bets were off.*

We are the strong ones; why are you acting like you're afraid of the bad guys?

> *So we were left with a simple decision: Either follow through on the commitment made by the last administration and leave Afghanistan, or say we*

> weren't leaving and commit another tens of thousands more troops going back to war.
>
> That was the choice — the real choice — between leaving or escalating.

Does President Biden think the general citizenry of the United States is stupid enough to believe there were only two choices, or does he actually believe it himself? Either way, this proposition of his displays a serious deficiency of the qualities required for leadership. If he lacked the mental acumen to conceive of more than two choices in this situation, then his judgement as Commander in Chief cannot be trusted. His lawful orders must still be followed under the authority of the Constitution for as long as he is President. But he cannot be trusted.

> *I was not going to extend this forever war, and I was not extending a forever exit.*

Utterly callous. Human beings were dying, *our friends,* and some were literally grasping onto airplanes out of desperation and falling to their deaths after takeoff. It reminded me of those poor trapped people who fell or jumped to their deaths from the Twin Towers – the war began and ended with similar horrifying images. Multitudes were dealing with the terror of their lives, and you're basically telling them, "Hurry up, I don't have time for this."

> *The decision to end the military airlift operations at Kabul airport was based on the unanimous recommendation of my civilian and military advisors — the Secretary of State, the Secretary of Defense, the Chairman of the Joint Chiefs of Staff and all the service chiefs, and the commanders in the field.*
>
> *Their recommendation was that the safest way to secure the passage of the remaining Americans and others out of the country was not to continue with 6,000 troops on the ground in harm's way in Kabul, but rather to get them out through non-military means.*

Great excuse! "Non-military means" is the way to go to rescue innocents from the enemy in time of war. All you have to do is declare the war over, and "Shazam!" No more need for military means.

Something about this situation above, as the President describes it, does not ring truthful to me. It just seems "off."

> *In the 17 days that we operated in Kabul after the Taliban seized power, we engaged in an around-the-*

> *clock effort to provide every American the opportunity to leave. Our State Department was working 24/7 contacting and talking, and in some cases, walking Americans into the airport.*
>
> *Again, more than 5,500 Americans were airlifted out. And for those who remain, we will make arrangements to get them out if they so choose.*

The aloof impatience, defeatism, and lack of motivation to save Americans is apparent throughout these comments. We'll just "make arrangements" without urgency against an enemy who has killed and maimed thousands of Americans.

> *As for the Afghans, we and our partners have airlifted 100,000 of them. No country in history has done more to airlift out the residents of another country than we have done. We will continue to work to help more people leave the country who are at risk. And we're far from done.*

One huge problem with such a rushed withdrawal is that we were not able to properly vet those we evacuated. An Afghan buddy of mine who is very plugged in to what's going on said, "There are sex offenders, thieves, thugs, predators, and people without any affiliation to the US or

Afghan government among the crowds around the airport." So how many of them had just enough of the right documentation to slip onboard a flight during the chaotic rush?

> *For now, I urge all Americans to join me in grateful prayer for our troops and diplomats and intelligence officers who carried out this mission of mercy in Kabul and at tremendous risk with such unparalleled results: an airma- — an airlift that evacuated tens of thousands to a network of volunteers and veterans who helped ~~identifies~~ [identify] those needing evacuation, guide them to the airport, and provided them for their support along the way.*
>
> *We're going to continue to need their help. We need your help. And I'm looking forward to meeting with you.*
>
> *And to everyone who is now offering or who will offer to welcome Afghan allies to their homes around the world, including in America: We thank you.*

Agreed. But these comments can be difficult to take coming from this particular source – like the previous example of the drunk driver who praises the EMS who came to save a

THE ESTABLISHMENT'S RESPONSE

family he himself rammed into, but who does not mention his own role in creating the tragedy. Yet, these words praising the heroes of the evacuation are true in themselves.

I take responsibility for the decision.

Weighty words. Which decision does he take responsibility for? The context seems to imply the decision for the timing of the mass evacuations within the short timeframe required to accommodate the artificial deadline he imposed, and which the Taliban was holding us to under threat.

If he truly takes responsibility for the mortal danger he put our troops and innocent civilians in, and for the international shame he brought onto America, and for the totality of the situation, his words need to be accompanied by action. In my opinion, the minimum action required to validate his words is his resignation from office. Historically, far harsher punishments have usually been meted out to losers of his ilk (I mean the term "loser" literally, not as a personal insult).

Now, some say we should have started mass evacuations sooner and "Couldn't this have be done — have been done in a more orderly manner?" I respectfully disagree.

Well now. I respectfully disagree with your respectful disagreement. See Section I.

> *Imagine if we had begun evacuations in June or July, bringing in thousands of American troops and evacuating more than 120,000 people in the middle of a civil war. There still would have been a rush to the airport, a breakdown in confidence and control of the government, and it still would have been a very difficult and dangerous mission.*

The above is only true in the circumstance where we abandon Afghanistan in the manner we did. The only variable he changed was the start of the evacuation, not any of the other factors discussed in Section I. This indicates that he is not up to the task of figuring things out, or that he rejects better ways of doing things because of an ingrained spirit of defeatism.

> *The bottom line is: There is no evacuatio- — evacuation from the end of a war that you can run without the kinds of complexities, challenges, and threats we faced. None.*

Certainly. I agree with you on this. Any type of end to a war has complexities, challenges and threats. That's why we need strong leaders of sound judgement.

THE ESTABLISHMENT'S RESPONSE

> *There are those who would say we should have stayed indefinitely for years on end. They ask, "Why don't we just keep doing what we were doing? Why did we have to change anything?"*

This is not relevant because recent Presidents of both parties determined that we were to withdraw our remaining forces. It was going to happen whether Trump or Biden was in office. Engaging with this contrary point of view distracts from the central issue of how the withdrawal was actually conducted.

> *The fact is: Everything had changed. My predecessor had made a deal with the Taliban. When I came into office, we faced a deadline — May 1. The Taliban onslaught was coming.*

This deal made by Biden's predecessor in office was not absolute, and was meant to respond to the conditions on the ground. In addition, the President uses a most disingenuous line of reasoning here, considering that he has worked to undo much else of what President Trump had put in place in every other sphere of the Executive Branch's authority.

"We faced a deadline" or else "the Taliban onslaught was coming." I suppose that the President believes that the spirit of American warfare is to run away? The defenders of Bastogne would have disagreed. "Nuts!"

> *We faced one of two choices: Follow the agreement of the previous administration and extend it to have — or extend to more time for people to get out; or send in thousands of more troops and escalate the war.*
>
> *To those asking for a third decade of war in Afghanistan, I ask: What is the vital national interest? In my view, we only have one: to make sure Afghanistan can never be used again to launch an attack on our homeland.*

Nobody I associate with and no serious person I am aware of is "asking for a third decade of war." As far as the question: "What is the vital national interest?" To which I ask in return: "Seriously?" If indeed he is serious, I implore President Biden and anybody with an interest in the good of the American nation to read Section III.

> *Remember why we went to Afghanistan in the first place? Because we were attacked by Osama bin Laden and al Qaeda on September 11th, 2001, and they were based in Afghanistan.*

True. You'll get no argument here.

THE ESTABLISHMENT'S RESPONSE

> *We delivered justice to bin Laden on May 2nd, 2011 — over a decade ago. Al Qaeda was decimated.*

As far as delivering justice to bin Laden, that needed to be done. He needed to be found and killed.

It was never the major point of the war, nor was decimating Al-Qaeda ever a "one and done" affair. You see, these Jihadists expect death. It's not that they go out of their way to expose themselves; otherwise, we never would have had to hunt for Osama. But they believe their cause to be bigger than themselves and their own death in the pursuit of it is not the worst thing they can imagine.

And in any case, bin Laden has achieved his dream. It had been his goal to drag us into a long and costly war that would end in our humiliation. He achieved it through Joseph Biden.

> *I respectfully suggest you ask yourself this question: If we had been attacked on September 11, 2001, from Yemen instead of Afghanistan, would we have ever gone to war in Afghanistan — even though the Taliban controlled Afghanistan in 2001? I believe the honest answer is "no."*

I have to ask you Mr. President, what's your point? The enemy headquarters for the operation that resulted in the

2001 September 11 attacks was located in Afghanistan, not Yemen. So of course, it was to Afghanistan that we went and not Yemen.

Oh, I see now. You're trying to say that the Taliban controlling Afghanistan is not a vital national interest in 2021 because we didn't think of it as a vital national interest before the 9/11 attacks. Taliban control of Afghanistan ain't really a bad thing, right?

Just take a look at Al-Qaeda. They are over the moon in exultation. They are resurgent, riding on the wings of their Taliban allies. This talk about decimating them a decade ago is not relevant to today's threats. But then again, I bet you believe we can win wars and eliminate terrorism with… drones.

Yes, that's the answer to all this. Drones.

That's because we had no vital national interest in Afghanistan other than to prevent an attack on America's homeland and their fr- — our friends. And that's true today.

Yes. That's supposed to be a **perpetual commitment**, by the way. You know, the Constitution's mandate to "provide for the common defence."

Oh, that's right, you think you can do it exclusively with drones. Gotcha.

In any case, concerning the previous government of Afghanistan that we fostered for decades – didn't they also count among our friends? Seems like they didn't get to have the attack on them prevented. In fact, they were hit in 2021 with, "a full-scale invasion, composed of Taliban, full Pakistani planning and logistical support, and at least 10-15,000 international terrorists, predominantly Pakistanis," as Afghan President Ghani related to the US President.

> *We succeeded in what we set out to do in Afghanistan over a decade ago. Then we stayed for another decade. It was time to end this war.*

By saying that "we succeeded in what we set out to do in Afghanistan over a decade ago," President Biden seems to be talking about the killing of bin Laden, as if that were the whole war. That would be at odds with his immediately preceding remark about our vital national interest being to prevent attacks on America and our friends.

Does he mean that bin Laden was the only main source of attacks? If so, that is plain wrong on its face.

Does he mean that the purpose of our incursion into central Asia was primarily to deliver justice to bin

Laden? This is also *completely wrong*. Hundreds of thousands of Americans deployed, tens of thousands of Americans casualties; none of that is justified simply to hunt down one man.

> *This is a new world. The terror threat has metastasized across the world, well beyond Afghanistan. We face threats from al-Shabaab in Somalia; al Qaeda affiliates in Syria and the Arabian Peninsula; and ISIS attempting to create a caliphate in Syria and Iraq, and establishing affiliates across Africa and Asia.*

The terror threat was never exclusively contained in Afghanistan, and we do truly face worldwide threats. This is why the campaigns dealing with it have fallen under the umbrella term "*Global* War on Terror" since the beginning. In themselves, these sentences above are true. But rhetorically, they are meant to place the idea in the listener's mind that Afghanistan had outlived its importance in the GWOT. This idea, of course, is false.

> *The fundamental obligation of a President, in my opinion, is to defend and protect America — not against threats of 2001, but against the threats of 2021 and tomorrow.*

Of course. But once again, it's ear candy – a rhetorical flourish devoid of underlying substance. Time traveling to 2001 is a moot issue. If the President were serious and competent about "the threats of 2021 and tomorrow" he would not have dismissed the importance of conducting the Afghan withdrawal from a position of dominance. He would not have set up the beleaguered but free government of the country to fail.

> *That is the guiding principle behind my decisions about Afghanistan. I simply do not believe that the safety and security of America is enhanced by continuing to deploy thousands of American troops and spending billions of dollars a year in Afghanistan.*
>
> *But I also know that the threat from terrorism continues in its pernicious and evil nature. But it's changed, expanded to other countries. Our strategy has to change too.*

Indeed, American strategy needs to be flexible to handle emerging threats. Keep in mind that confronting terror in other countries does not logically imply allowing terror to return to preeminence in Afghanistan. President Biden is illogically implying this to be the case.

> *We will maintain the fight against terrorism in Afghanistan and other countries.*

Really? So… You fight terrorism by surrendering to it? **Because you just allowed terrorism to conquer that entire nation.** Perhaps you have better ways to "maintain the fight" than to try winning it.

> *We just don't need to fight a ground war to do it. We have what's called over-the-horizon capabilities, which means we can strike terrorists and targets without American boots on the ground — or very few, if needed.*

Oh wow! That seems so magical. President Wilson had "The War to End All Wars" and President Biden has "The Capabilities to End All Terrorism." I suppose we are blessed to have such a bottle of snake oil sitting on the desk of the Oval Office.

> *We've shown that capacity just in the last week. We struck ISIS-K remotely, days after they murdered 13 of our servicemembers and dozens of innocent Afghans.*

Now we get to taste the snake oil. The brand name is *Drones.*

THE ESTABLISHMENT'S RESPONSE

> It is rather peculiar to respond to a terrorist attack that killed innocent Afghans by killing more innocent Afghans. But that is exactly what President Biden did. This result too, was foreseeable. The limitations of drone strikes have been known for some time. There are many good and militarily beneficial things that drones can do. They are indeed amazing pieces of technology. But they do not win wars.

> *And to ISIS-K: We are not done with you yet.*

My eyes widened in astonishment when he said this. The video of the speech has to be viewed and listened to in order to get the full effect. This line and the way he delivered it has to rank as the most uninspiring, insipid, and impotent warning to a terrorist group I have ever heard.

> *As Commander-in-Chief, I firmly believe the best path to guard our safety and our security lies in a tough, unforgiving, targeted, precise strategy that goes after terror where it is today, not where it was two decades ago. That's what's in our national interest.*

Okay. But you're still not addressing the central issue – the betrayal of Afghanistan and America's 9/11 legacy.

> *And here's a critical thing to understand: The world is changing. We're engaged in a serious competition with China. We're dealing with the challenges on multiple fronts with Russia. We're confronted with cyberattacks and nuclear proliferation.*

President Biden has immeasurably strengthened China and possibly Russia through our humiliation, and through the rich provision of our best equipment and the mineral resources of Afghanistan to China. The same could also plausibly apply to Russia and Iran.

> *We have to shore up America's competitive[ness] to meet these new challenges in the competition for the 21st century. And we can do both: fight terrorism and take on new threats that are here now and will continue to be here in the future.*

> *And there's nothing China or Russia would rather have, would want more in this competition than the United States to be bogged down another decade in Afghanistan.*

China and Russia, as well as Al-Qaeda, the Taliban, and ISIS-K, ended up far better under the current arrangement than they ever could have in almost any other imagined scenario, even if we were to be "bogged down another decade." Not that that would have happened, since large troop commitments were coming to an end regardless of the US political party in charge.

But I do not believe China or Russia could possibly have masterminded anything better than what they have now. Of course, they will continue forward with their aggression, aided by the tremendous material and moral boost they received due to the malfeasance of the American leadership.

> As we turn the page on the foreign policy that has guided our nat- — our nation the last two decades, we've got to learn from our mistakes.
>
> To me, there are two that are paramount. First, we must set missions with clear, achievable goals — not ones we'll never reach. And second, we must stay clearly focused on the fundamental national security interest of the United States of America.

These sentiments are nothing unique to Joe Biden. But they are sensible.

> This decision about Afghanistan is not just about Afghanistan. It's about ending an era of major military operations to remake other countries.

Still skipping the central issue of the way the withdrawal was conducted, and the layers of betrayal it consisted of.

> *We saw a mission of counterterrorism in Afghanistan — getting the terrorists and stopping attacks — morph into a counterinsurgency, nation building — trying to create a democratic, cohesive, and unified Afghanistan -- something that has never been done over the many centuries of ~~Afghans'~~ [Afghanistan's] history.*

Almost everyone is in agreement on this. At least that demonstrates some minimal progress towards national consensus.

> *Moving on from that mindset and those kind of large-scale troop deployments will make us stronger and more effective and safer at home.*

This is potentially true, depending on the leadership and prudential judgement of those in charge.

> *And for anyone who gets the wrong idea, let me say it clearly. To those who wish America harm, to those that engage in terrorism against us and our allies, know this: The United States will never rest. We will not forgive. We will not forget. We will hunt you*

> *down to the ends of the Earth, and we will — you will pay the ultimate price.*

You don't get the Jihadist mentality if you don't understand that Jihadists expect to die in their holy war. Your words are not a threat to them, even if they were true. My impression is they are not.

There is little or nothing genuinely inspiring in President Biden's delivery, and his actions have been directly counter to his words. *He threw a war.*

> *And let me be clear: We will continue to support the Afghan people through diplomacy, international influence, and humanitarian aid. We'll continue to push for regional diplomacy and engagement to prevent violence and instability. We'll continue to speak out for basic rights of the Afghan people, especially women and girls, as we speak out for women and girls all around the globe. And I've been clear that human rights will be the center of our foreign policy.*

Utterly meaningless because you **already had the chance to prove it. The real test was now.** This is like the married philanderer who tells his wife, "*C'mon man*, this time it'll be different."

> *But the way to do that is not through endless military deployments, but through diplomacy, economic tools, and rallying the rest of the world for support.*

These non-military means should come first, absolutely. The military should be a last resort. But it should at least be on the table as an option. That's why it exists; some countries out there are real threats and would love to *kill Americans*.

And if you're serious about rallying the rest of the world to our support, your credibility is shot because of the visible and very public betrayal of Afghanistan and America's 9/11 legacy.

> *My fellow Americans, the war in Afghanistan is now over. I'm the fourth President who has faced the issue of whether and when to end this war. When I was running for President, I made a commitment to the American people that I would end this war. And today, I've honored that commitment. It was time to be honest with the American people again. We no longer had a clear purpose in an open-ended mission in Afghanistan.*
>
> *After 20 years of war in Afghanistan, I refused to send another generation of America's sons and*

> *daughters to fight a war that should have ended long ago.*

More fluff. Ending a war does not mean sabotaging our side. Are you ever going to give a sufficient explanation for that?

> *After more than $2 trillion spent in Afghanistan — a cost that researchers at Brown University estimated would be over $300 million a day for 20 years in Afghanistan — for two decades — yes, the American people should hear this: $300 million a day for two decades.*
>
> *If you take the number of $1 trillion, as many say, that's still $150 million a day for two decades. And what have we lost as a consequence in terms of opportunities? I refused to continue in a war that was **no longer in the service of the vital national interest of our people.***

Some type of American oversight of **Afghanistan was and is absolutely in the vital national interest of our people**, as Section III clearly explains. As far as the monetary issue: Once again, nearly everyone was in agreement that the war had cost too much money. Taxpayer dollars were bankrolling corruption and even filtered over to terrorists.

This was a despicable evil in itself. It did not logically follow that the solution was to sabotage those things that were good and were already in place that had some "modicum of success." Indeed, it is utterly contrary to logic to destroy that which is built when there is no need to do so. The ironic thing is that now we really are more likely to pay a lot more, both in money and blood.

> *And most of all, after 800,000 Americans serving in Afghanistan — I've traveled that whole country — brave and honorable service; after 20,744 American servicemen and women injured, and the loss of 2,461 American personnel, including 13 lives lost just this week, I refused to open another decade of warfare in Afghanistan.*

Nobody asked him to open another decade of warfare. The informed American will recognize that this is a strawman argument. Most citizens would have been okay with an honorable exit that did not put the United States in greater danger. I find it incredible that he cites statistics of veteran numbers and combat casualties as a justification for dishonoring those very veterans and casualties – the real life American heroes behind the numbers.

THE ESTABLISHMENT'S RESPONSE

We've been a nation too long at war. If you're 20 years old today, you have never known an America at peace.

Indeed, 20 was the most common age (the mode) of the 13 who were killed on 26 August; four of our departed heroes were 20 years old.

So, when I hear that we could've, should've continued the so-called low-grade effort in Afghanistan, at low risk to our service members, at low cost, I don't think enough people understand how much we have asked of the 1 percent of this country who put that uniform on, who are willing to put their lives on the line in defense of our nation.

Maybe it's because my deceased son, Beau, served in Iraq for a full year, before that. Well, maybe it's because of what I've seen over the years as senator, vice president, and president traveling these countries.

A lot of our veterans and their families have gone through hell — deployment after deployment, months and years away from their families; missed birthdays, anniversaries; empty chairs at holidays;

financial struggles; divorces; loss of limbs; traumatic brain injury; posttraumatic stress.

We see it in the struggles many have when they come home. We see it in the strain on their families and caregivers. We see it in the strain of their families when they're not there. We see it in the grief borne by their survivors. The cost of war they will carry with them their whole lives.

Most tragically, we see it in the shocking and stunning statistic that should give pause to anyone who thinks war can ever be low-grade, low-risk, or low-cost: 18 veterans, on average, who die by suicide every single day in America — not in a far-off place, but right here in America.

You made all of the above so much worse by betraying their legacy. Perhaps exponentially worse.

There's nothing low-grade or low-risk or low-cost about any war.

Of course! The small gains in Afghanistan were bought at a high price and you demolished what little we did accomplish. Why do you think so many are upset?

It's time to end the war in Afghanistan.

THE ESTABLISHMENT'S RESPONSE

The issue here is not about ending the war or not. It's about *how* you ended American involvement. This cannot be downplayed, minimized or overlooked. It's the difference between a prisoner of war who gives up and cooperates with the enemy and a prisoner of war who, despite his unfavorable situation, **continues to resist the enemy in the best way he can**. That is the difference between heroes and cowards.

> *As we close 20 years of war and strife and pain and sacrifice, it's time to look to the future, not the past — to a future that's safer, to a future that's more secure, to a future that honors those who served and all those who gave what President Lincoln called their "last full measure of devotion."*

Alas, another phase of strife and pain has been inaugurated, and this is the future you have just begun to give us. Even if we get through this upcoming era without further calamity, so much lasting damage has been done. And we do not yet fully grasp the second and third order consequences bursting out from the Pandora's box of your pullout sellout.

> *I give you my word: With all of my heart, I believe this is the right decision, a wise decision, and the best decision for America. Thank you. Thank you.*

Mr. President, with all of *my* heart, and from the deepest interior of my soul, I regret to relate that my conscience will not permit me to tell you that you are welcome.

And may God bless you all. And may God protect our troops.

Amen. Sigh…

And that concludes his speech.

I pray that gold has started to peel off from the brick, and that the underlying foolishness, spin, and outright deceit are at least somewhat more apparent.

The following day, on September 1, SecDef Austin and Chairman of the Joint Chiefs GEN Milley gave a joint press briefing. The full transcript can be found on *defense.gov*.

There was really no earthshattering new information, though SecDef Austin did make some acknowledgement of the outrage felt by servicemembers:

> *But we shouldn't expect Afghan war veterans to agree anymore than any other group of Americans. I've heard strong views from many sides in recent days, and that's vital, that's democracy, that's America. As we always do, this department will look*

> *back clearly and professionally and learn every lesson that we can. That's our way.*

GEN Milley's comments included a lot of the dry details of what happened without much commentary of substance.

As a side point, I'd like to remind everyone that that's why I only included enough detail in this book to make the necessary points, but no more. Exact statistics on equipment lost, evacuees in various categories, and so forth, as well as the precise chronological minutiae of events is all information that is readily available with a careful internet search. In its own way, that stuff is fascinating in itself. However, I have found that these details tend to provide a lot of weightless fluff that fills time and takes up space on pages when all that is needed is to get to a substantive point.

And so, GEN Milley went on in a "fluffy" manner at the press briefing. But at the very end, he made some heavy comments that deserve to be looked at:

> *So, Barb, you asked me where my pain and anger comes from. I have all of those same emotions and I'm sure the Secretary does and I'm -- any -- anyone who's served. And -- and I commanded troops and I wasn't born a four star General. I have walked*

> *through patrols and been blown up and shot at and RPG'd and everything else. My pain and anger comes from the same as the grieving families, the same as those soldiers that are on the ground.*
>
> *Last night, I visited the wounded up in Walter Reed. This is tough stuff. War is hard, it's vicious, it's brutal, it's unforgiving, and yes, we all have pain and anger. And when we see what has unfolded over the last 20 years and over the last 20 days, that creates pain and anger, and mine comes from 242 of my soldiers killed in action over 20 years in Iraq and Afghanistan.*

I find his comments about his pain and anger to be believable. Most combat veterans can identify. Why then, GEN Milley, if your pain comes from the loss of the gallant Soldiers under your command who were killed in action, *why* did you assist the very Jihadist enemies who killed those Soldiers?

The distinct impression I get from his following comment is that it was a false sense of duty that led him into a situation of intense cognitive dissonance, one that he was not able to resolve in favor of the United States and its Constitution.

So yeah, I have that. But I'm a professional soldier. I'm going to contain my pain and anger and continue to execute my mission.

These words genuinely represent the values of a professional Soldier. But as with so much that has occurred in this period of time, it does not properly apply here because of the situation's extra-ordinary nature.

Your mission can never be to give aid and comfort to our enemies. If your Commander in Chief orders you to do so, that is an unlawful order. Indeed, to follow such an order violates the Law of the Land itself – it's unconstitutional.

You *know* that you not only don't have to follow it, but that you are *not permitted* to follow it. "Not authorized" as the military verbiage usually puts it. If you do follow such an unconstitutional order from the President, you yourself are culpably complicit.

II. HELPFUL ARTICLES

Choi, Joseph. "Afghan interpreter who helped extract Biden, other senators in 2008 asks President to save him." *The Hill*, August 31, 2021.

Milburn, Andrew. "Opinion: Defense Secretary Lloyd Austin must resign." *Task and Purpose*, October 13, 2021.

---. "A shabby ending: The US flight from Afghanistan was a mistake." *Military Times*, July 9, 2021.

Nelson, Steven. "Biden droned the wrong guy, innocent aid worker killed in Kabul strike: NYT." *New York Post*, September 10, 2021.

---. "Psaki says Biden nixed 9/11 Afghan deadline because military needed just 120 days." *New York Post*, August 31, 2021.

Pannet, Rachel, Erin Cunningham, Jennifer Hassan, and Claire Parker. "U.S. troops will remain in Afghanistan until all American citizens are evacuated, Biden tells ABC News." *The Washington Post*, August 18, 2021.

"Why is August 31 the date for the US pullout from Afghanistan?" (AFP). *France 24*, August 25, 2021.

III. WHY EVERY AMERICAN SHOULD BE CONCERNED

The "modicum of success" that had been achieved in Afghanistan was limited, but it was worth preserving, if only to prevent the disaster that we are now seeing. This limited, unsteady stalemate was the only tangible memorial of the sacrifices of our troops. It may not have seemed like much on the outside, but it was the wall that was holding back the diabolical expansion of Jihadist and Communist power.

There are no Taliban troops on American soil. So, life goes on for the overwhelming majority. This is not to say there are no covert Jihadists around, but there is no overt occupation.

Yet, the Afghan withdrawal has revealed a number of issues which are of *the gravest concern* – "vital national interests," as the phrase goes. The first two on this list deal with deeply embedded systemic problems in the establishment's mindset that have been exposed with a floodlight by the Afghan debacle.

The four which follow are broad categories of lasting damage that has been caused by the great sabotage. Preventing these from happening was more than enough justification for us to withdraw with strength, on our terms, while continuing to support the free Afghan forces against the Jihadist takeover.

1) Ignorance of the fundamental need for victory.

2) Failure to understand the enemy.

3) Destructive effect of defeatism on veterans and families.

4) Abandonment and betrayal of allies (a.k.a. Loss of honor, reputation).

5) Strengthening of terrorism.

6) Communist China's proxy victory, through:

   A - Reverse engineering of US military technology

   B - Gaining access to Afghanistan's untapped mineral riches

   C - Boxing in or "bracketing" India, a friend and emerging power

   D - Emboldening of aggression, with regard to Taiwan and others

"We must make sure nothing like this ever happens again."

Alas, sentiments like this abound. I have heard Congressmen saying such things on radio and television interviews, and similar notions have been expressed by others I know personally and have spoken to, both in the military and out.

I certainly empathize. After all, what else could one say after such tragedy – that we must make sure something like this *does* happen again? *Duh*, of course not. That would be preposterous. We only have the future to work with.

But really, the train has left the station, the horse has bolted from the stable, the chicken has flown the coop. Choose your own old saying or cliché, the point remains the same.

One more well-worn phrase will explain why this is so. *Three strikes and you're out.*

Vietnam was strike one.

Iraq was strike two. (For those who like baseball analogies: It may have been a foul ball instead of a swing-and-a-miss, but it still counts as a strike).

Afghanistan is strike three.

We had every opportunity to do a proper post-mortem on Vietnam, and by golly, we collectively sure did. Entire libraries worth of books were written in the decades after the war, covering every conceivable angle of the Vietnam experience, and usually with some kind of pedagogical undertone. Something like, "Lookee here, we did this and that wrong, we've identified problems and proposed solutions, and now we're in a better place to forge into the future if we remember the lessons of this era."

Fair enough. In fact, it would be indicative of an insipid society not worthy of continuing existence if it *didn't* do some serious self-introspection. But given the lack of different results, were all these "after action reviews" a fool's errand?

1. IGNORANCE OF THE FUNDAMENTAL NEED FOR VICTORY

"*You have written your own history and have written it in red on your enemies' breast.*"

This is what General Douglas MacArthur told the assembled throng of the 165th Infantry, previously (and currently) known as the 69th, on the eve of the United States formally getting into the fight in World War II. Inherent in the quote is the idea that victory is glory, and the only result that justifies the risk of one's life is the triumph of one's cause.

The Taliban and other Jihadist groups understand this, perhaps to an insane extreme. The junior servicemembers of the US Armed Forces generally understand this, particularly in the combat arms. Our senior leadership does not seem to understand this.

General Milley, now the head of the Joint Chiefs, used to have a great reputation. While I never served with him, some friends of mine have, and he was always held in high regard, until 2020 when he started to go in an overtly political direction in public.

I was speaking with such a friend, who is also well versed in military matters.

I had to ask him, "What the *bleep* is going on with General Milley? I used to hold him in high regard, but my respect for him has plummeted in the past year or so."

His answer is as informative as it is humorous: "His careerism expanded as his waist line did."

Concerning the trio of Austin, Milley, and McKenzie, retired Marine Special Ops Colonel Andrew Milburn had this to say in a *Task and Purpose* opinion piece titled, "Defense Secretary Lloyd Austin must resign":

"I consider all three to be honorable men whom I know to have sacrificed much for their country. But I cannot fathom how three prominent men could serve a profession for some 120 years between them, and yet so fundamentally misinterpret the moral and intellectual demands of that same profession."

The troops will not respect a senior leader if it's obvious that the leader has little regard for the troops. Servicemembers do not want to be coddled, but they do want to be respected as men and women and led to success.

Indeed, a certain democratic spirit in the ranks of the military cannot be stopped. To make it clear, we are not talking about undisciplined mob rule or even anything formal.

We are speaking of those intangible qualities - respect, regard, esteem. When these are lost by those in the highest positions, men like Marine Lieutenant Colonel Stuart Scheller step to the front to fill the gap in our defenses. Indeed, honorable leadership that cares for the troops and leads them to success in the mission is the very skin that defends the internal organs from exposure to infectious pathogens.

LtCol Scheller publicly spoke out to call for accountability from senior leadership by posting a video that went viral. This was in the wake of the August 26, 2021, suicide bombing which killed hundreds packed at the edge of the Kabul Airport – including 13 US servicemembers, most of whom were Marines.

Of course, the establishment retaliated and fired him, then arrested him.

He also received his fair share of criticism from erstwhile peers; the comments below are taken from an online military forum I belong to:

"You cannot challenge your entire Chain of Command in public in front of your subordinates. He knew what would happen I'm sure."

"Use the chain of command. Not social media. As a Commander, his *job* is to preserve it, not grandstand. I'm not going to get into his [*Scheller's*] "analysis" which is flat out wrong."

"Totally unprofessional behavior. Whether you agree with his point of view or not this is wrong. It has done damage to the military profession. And it will be even more wrong when right wing/conservative groups make him out as a hero.

> He violated his oath and he is not a hero by any means."

> "I agree with a lot of what he said, but you still don't publicly call out your leaders like that, especially in uniform."

Certainly, in a circumstance that's not a constitutional crisis, all of the above applies. But I don't believe that the people who made the above comments have grasped the *existential* enormity of the problem, of the organizational rot that causes a bloated institution to be blind to the purpose of its own existence. I believe they still are focused on arranging the deck chairs after the iceberg has been struck.

Others, however, get it:

> "I find it interesting he has lost the trust of his superiors for the same action that gained him the trust of his peers, subordinates, and most of the Republic he serves."

Stu Scheller gained many, many supporters. It was not only Marines he inspired; servicemembers from across the Armed Forces were able to identify with the demand for accountability he was giving voice to. For instance, Brianna Puff, an Airman I had served with on a joint mission, had this to say: "THIS is a leader. THIS is an officer I would proudly serve under. THIS is what more senior leaders should aspire to be like."

The following are excerpts of the statement that LtCol Stuart Scheller read in court when he faced charges stemming from his public calls for accountability in leadership. They hit home with force:

> "I was thinking about the parallels of Vietnam and Afghanistan as I read General Berger's letter to the Force dated 18 August. This letter in my opinion perfectly illustrates **senior military leader's** [sic] **inability to see the true pain in Service members following a failed war effort.** General Berger told Service members their sacrifices were worth it without offering any connection back to a bigger purpose. He concluded the letter with how Service members should go seek counseling. At no point did he acknowledge any failures of the leadership…"

> "In that moment I had clarity. I realized the military was continuing to make the same mistakes because senior leaders continued to diagnose the wrong problem. I concluded that our senior leaders were either unable or unwilling to have an honest

discussion about our failures in a public forum that would necessitate REAL change."

There are many, both pro- and anti-Scheller, who are of the opinion that he should have addressed these concerns within the chain of command. In ordinary circumstances, absolutely, no question. But these were extra-ordinary circumstances. He had already determined that that would be a dead end.

"I also decided that quietly addressing these concerns within the chain of command would be ineffective."

"In the first video, "**The reason people are so upset right now is NOT because of the Marine on the battlefield.** That Service member has always rose to the occasion and done extraordinary things. **The reason people are so upset right now is because their senior leaders let them down**, and none of them are raising their hands and taking accountability."

"I wasn't mentally unstable, just very angry at what I perceived to be consistent **betrayal**."

"My statements all center around the fact that **I do not believe General Officers are held to the same**

> **standards as junior leaders.** I also believe, that similar to post Vietnam, the Marine Corps leadership is trying to spin the narrative about our failures on the junior enlisted without taking a hard look at themselves."

To our elected officials: Do you notice the recurring themes in what we concerned veterans are saying?

Combat Soldiers, and other servicemembers, can put up with a lot if they know they are being led in the *direction* of triumph. Nobody can tell the future, so you don't know exactly how it will turn out, but as long as leaders are leading in the direction of triumph, morale (and mental health down the road) will be maintained.

Fr. Duffy tells us about the troops of the 42nd "Rainbow" Division (MacArthur's own) after the bloody Battle of the Ourcq in July of 1918:

> "I have become a specialist on what they call the morale of troops and as I go around I find that the morale of the men in this division is still very high. They have had a tough week of it and nearly half the infantry are gone while of those remaining more than half are sick. But they know that they have whipped the enemy on his chosen ground…"

Leadership that leads to success in the mission, to VICTORY, is the only acceptable kind of leadership. Otherwise, what is the point of putting yourself in mortal danger?

Careerism is the cancer, one that leads to blindness to the fundamental need for victory. The Afghan debacle has revealed how deeply it has infected the upper echelons of our Armed Forces, and it would be appropriate for all citizens to feel deeply uneasy about it.

2. FAILURE TO UNDERSTAND THE ENEMY

A buddy I served in Afghanistan with, Donald Loveland, had this to say about our COIN (Counter-Insurgency Operations) and the end result in Afghanistan: "Driving around giving hugs… to the enemy didn't help us in the end. Seems like mission priority has shifted from lethality and competence to wokeness. This is all on the leadership"

There are so many failures in regard to understanding the nature of the enemy and how he thinks that it could take volumes to properly capture in full detail. It was not necessarily that the foe we faced in central Asia was so peculiar. The meta-issue is the systemic problem in

American thinking that fails to understand how others view us and how they fight us.

For example, threatening Jihadist terrorists with vows that we're going to get them does not really do much. *They expect to die.*

And, has anyone in the upper echelons heard of *Pashtunwali*? This is the unwritten constitution of the Pashtun people, an uncodified oral law that they live by. The Pashtuns are the ethnic group whose geographical territory occupies southern and eastern Afghanistan and the adjacent mountain regions of Pakistan.

The Taliban are almost exclusively derived from the Pashtuns. This is not to say that all Pashtuns are Taliban or supporters, but almost all Taliban and supporters are Pashtun.

Pashtunwali demands vengeance.

If you kill one of them, his brothers, sons, cousins, etc. will make it their mission in life to kill you and those associated with you.

The Taliban had already hated America on ideological grounds before 2001. But since we swept into central Asia after the three thousand Americans were murdered on the 11th of September in that fateful year, we have paid the Taliban back many times over. The US-led NATO forces utterly devastated the Jihadist group over two decades, slaughtering them by the tens of thousands. *Tens of thousands*. Killed. Dead.

The Taliban may have won the war, but it was costly for them. That's a lot of vengeance stewing in the crock pot.

Fast forward to 26 August, to the suicide blast that killed 13 US servicemembers. It was the parting shot of the Jihadists in this long, painful journey. In President Biden's speeches, he was always at pains to emphasize the distinction between the Taliban and ISIS-K, and to leave no doubt that it was ISIS-K who did the deed, and that they were the "sworn enemies of the Taliban."

Did it occur to him or members of his Administration that whatever beef these two groups have with each other, they both hate America even more? The Taliban knew that US forces had the ability to retaliate with "extreme prejudice" if given the green light, and they were not so cocky as to openly poke the bear, yet. They carry vengeance in their hearts, but they needed plausible deniability *just in case* President Biden showed some moxie. It really was not much for the Taliban to give a wink and a nod to Islamic State members and let them do their thing, and then after the attack to blame the Americans for allowing the security failure.

All this talk by President Biden about not being done with ISIS-K yet, about not forgiving and forgetting, and hunting them down – beyond the languid delivery of these lines, I do not find his declared commitment to be believable. Perhaps there will be some flourishes for show, some wagging of the dog to demonstrate a superficial strength, but I do not foresee a genuinely effective anti-terrorist policy.

For crying out loud, he just handed terrorists their greatest victory in two decades!

Furthermore, even if a policy is implemented that succeeds in the stated goal of hunting down ISIS-K, this does not stop them. *Jihadists expect their own deaths.*

Air Force veteran Ian Fritz wrote a fascinating article in *The Atlantic* ("What I learned while eavesdropping on the Taliban") in which he describes some of his unique work as a military linguist. The following excerpt is revealing:

> "I watched fighter jets drop 500-pound bombs into the middle of a battle, turning 20 men into dust. As I took in the new landscape, full of craters instead

of people, there was a lull in the noise, and I thought, *Surely now we've killed enough of them.* We hadn't...

And as I watched six Americans die, what felt like 20 Taliban rejoiced in my ears, "Waaaaallahu akbar, they're dying!"

It didn't matter that they were unarmored men, with 30-year-old guns, fighting against gunships, fighter jets, helicopters, and a far-better-equipped ground team. It also didn't matter that 100 of them died that day. Through all that noise, the sounds of bombs and bullets exploding behind them, their fellow fighters being killed, the Taliban kept their spirits high, kept encouraging one another, kept insisting that not only were they winning, but that they'd get us again—even better—next time."

Killing *any* Americans was a victory to them, no matter what their own casualties were. This has proven to be a pretty ubiquitous feature of Jihadist movements.

Kill them we must, but *just* killing them will ultimately not permanently defeat them. It may be necessary for victory, but is not sufficient. What is needed for *decisive* and *permanent* VICTORY is to **eradicate the**

Jihadist movements themselves. I fully admit, that's easier said than done.

I'm sure some of you have noticed the conundrum that is created by the two traits of Pashtun culture and martial ethos touched on here. To repel their attacks, we have to kill them and keep killing them, or else they will keep coming. And yet, killing them is what spurs their multitudinous relations to swear vengeance and sign up to kill Americans!

What we have is a self-reinforcing cycle of violence, one that has been propagating from one generation to the next from time immemorial. Is it really any surprise that the region is so messed up, or that the results of America's intervention were less than stellar?

We really have a lot to learn.

3. DESTRUCTIVE EFFECT OF DEFEATISM ON VETERANS AND FAMILIES

The esteem in which leaders are held, and their corollary ability to bring their charges to victory, has an effect that determines real results. War can stir the greatest qualities an individual has. On the other hand, frivolously dispensing with the sacrifices of the troops has a distinctly harmful effect on those who served on the front line.

This is what has happened, and American society is paying and will continue to pay for the unnecessary trauma inflicted on veterans on the home front. Even to begin with, "war is hell," as General Sherman famously declared. A cynical attitude that takes defeat for granted, and sees no problem with it, will inflict that much more trauma on our veteran population, almost certainly with a cascading multi-generational effect. America has enough problems; we really did not need this one imposed on us by our leaders.

The traditional American attitude was expressed by one of the greatest Generals of all time, George S. Patton III. He spoke to the Third Army, which he commanded, and his legendary speech is depicted in the 1970 movie *Patton*, which turned him into a household name for a new generation:

> "Americans love a winner and will not tolerate a loser. Americans play to win all the time. Now, I wouldn't give a hoot in hell for a man who lost and laughed. That's why Americans have never lost and will never lose a war. Because the very thought of losing is hateful to Americans."

How far we have come.

Perhaps it was a merciful favor from above for Patton that he didn't live to see his bold prognosis for the future dashed away by a different reality. Different kinds of people were rising to the top in political leadership.

Not many years after the film *Patton* came out, a fellow named Joe Biden started his public career by doing his part to demolish the achievements American servicemen had fought and died for over the previous decade.

The Republic of Vietnam, "South" Vietnam, was mostly free as of 1973. It was fraught with problems, certainly, but it had a large military that was well-trained to fight in the expensive Western manner. With the help of the United States, it had withstood continuous Communist assault over the previous decade.

When the US withdrew its last troops in 1973, the deal was that we'd have the back of the South Vietnamese. We would continue to help them with funding and technical support, and any big moves on the part of the North would be dealt with severely. That deal was worked out under President Nixon. A "peace with honor."

Except, the President ended up losing credibility at home because of the Watergate scandal, and resigned in

1974. Shortly thereafter, Congress voted to defund the Republic of Vietnam. We no longer had troops there and the country had been holding on with our moral support, so pulling the plug at this time was inexplicable.

For an explanation, please ask the current President. This vote was one of the earliest acts of his national political career. As former Conservative Party Senator from NY James Buckley pointed out in his account *If Men Were Angels*, the denial of military aid to South Vietnam not only sealed its fate, but was not a kneejerk vote – there was sufficient deliberation for all the Senators to know what they were doing.

Anti-American defeatism runs deep in the Biden psyche, and Vietnam, as long ago as it was, lingers with us. President Biden is the historical link; he was a part of promoting defeat in that war, and he did it again in our own era as the Commander in Chief of the Armed Forces of the United States.

A couple of days before the middle of August, 2021, I had the opportunity to speak again to J.P. Lawrence of *Stars and Stripes*. He was doing a follow-up to his article on the subject from the previous year, and things were falling apart now faster than anyone expected:

J.P. - The Taliban have taken 18 out of the 34 provinces, all in a week.

How do you feel about this, how does this news make you feel?

SÉAMUS - My feelings on this now are identical to the feelings I had when we spoke one year ago, when you wrote that article for the 19th anniversary of the terrorist attacks of 2001/09/11.

The only distinction in my outlook between then and now is the **increased sense of betrayal** similar to what I felt in 2011 or so when the US completely pulled out of Iraq, setting the stage for the Islamic State. In this case, the US ceased combat operations in 2014.

We were not even so deeply involved in regular ground combat in recent years that we could say we were too involved in Afghanistan. The American role was in keeping a lid on things, preserving the gains that had been made - namely, we prevented Afghan. from being used as a base for the spread of Islamist terrorism.

A complete pullout is not only unnecessary, it is sabotage - a betrayal of American and

international forces who have expended so much in life and limb to prevent the resurgence of the Taliban.

I am disgusted.

The following four days were absolute chaos. The whole Afghan project was imploding before our eyes. I had the opportunity to passionately but rationally voice my concerns on national TV. I did an in-studio interview for CNN's New Day with host John Berman, who was an absolute gentleman. This is from the morning of August 17; the Taliban had only just taken over Kabul, and it was not entirely clear how much they occupied. The collapse of the country was still a new thing:

> BERMAN - Look, we just heard President Biden, what he said yesterday, and I know you've been watching the images from Afghanistan like the rest of us have over the last few days. What does that feel like for you?
>
> SÉAMUS - It's heartbreaking. It's a mixture of both anger and sadness. And that principally derives from, one, the human tragedy of it all, just as a gut reaction, but also the unnecessity of it.

Now, we're not talking big picture strategy. There were many forks in the road over the past 20 years, what could have been done. Turn left, turn right.

What we're talking about right now is an extremely hasty withdrawal where the cord was pulled out from the Afghan forces and their ability to defend their country. And proper provision was not made for those who allied themselves with us, who placed their entire trust in the United States to protect them and their families.

And I have personal experience with this right now. I can't give names, but there are people behind the scenes, Afghans, who have come over, who are trying to get their families out because they know that they will be slaughtered by the Taliban once the Taliban takes over complete control of the country.

And this is something that's happening right here, right now. It's real. The feelings are visceral. They come from the gut because it's an actual human tragedy that's happening right now. And like I said, it's so preventable because we trained the Afghan forces to fight in our manner, which was a very technology dependent manner, one that relied on airpower. And then yank those very resources away that we trained them to be dependent on.

At this point, things were worse than anyone could imagine. But they were to become even worse yet.

After the August 26 suicide bombing in Kabul that killed 11 Marines, a Soldier, and a Sailor, it really hurt to hear the justified anger of my friends. The hurt came, I think, from knowing that all the words of vengeance and fist shaking at the bad guys was ultimately just empty posturing. For instance, calling the attack an "act of war" was moot. We were already at war. And our big boss was forfeiting it.

The impotence of the supreme Commander reminds me of the man who curls up into a ball during a fair fist fight, cowering in the corner while pleading, "No, don't hurt me!" He earns no respect because he did not stand up for himself. Indeed, he invites scorn.

If he is a nasty coward, he invites even more scorn. Imagine a loud-mouthed wimp getting beat up. Then, as he lies bloody, bruised, and immobile on the ground, he yells out to the victor who is walking away, "I'm gonna kick the *bleep* out of you!"

Onlookers can't help but to laugh at the absurdity. The victor simply raises his eyebrows, smirks, and says, "Yeah guy, whatever," as he strolls off.

The problem with having a President who has a personality like the craven loud-mouthed wimp above is that he's the pilot of the plane. Those of us who believe in duty, honor, and country are forced to go along for a fatally painful ride.

Truly, the way veterans are treated by those who send them to war has a profound effect on them personally, but also on their families. The following comments to Andrew Wilkow sharply express the pain of Kathy McCollum, mother of Marine Corps Lance Cpl. Rylee J. McCollum who was killed in the Kabul Airport blast of 26 August: "Twenty years and 6 months old, getting ready to go home from freaking Jordan to be home with his wife to watch the birth of his son, and that feckless, dementia-ridden piece of crap just sent my son to die."

I cannot emphasize enough that the leadership must have the "six" of their troops. We covered how pursuit of victory is essential and must be strived for. Defeatism, the flip side, is absolutely destructive and must be avoided. Defeatism, as a concept, does not deal with a defeat that's suffered after a true best effort, but rather is a cynical attitude towards winning, a certain jaded negativity that emphasizes the futility of a given project.

It is positively destructive.

Most combat veterans adjust well to normal life after the service. Post-Traumatic Stress symptoms are actually totally normal. But Post-Traumatic Stress *Disorder* is bound to afflict a certain percentage. This is where the leadership has the greatest opportunity to be of help by *not* doing the defeatist things that inflame the crisis.

Jonathan Shay, M.D., has written brilliantly about PTSD in the context of Vietnam and the ancient Iliad and Odyssey of Homer. He shows that post-combat trauma is not some new phenomenon, but can be detected in the most ancient tales out there. Human psychology was the same 70 years ago, 3,000 years ago, or 50,000 years ago, and it responds to certain stimuli in predictable ways.

Rob Paterson, a member of a military forum I belong to, posted this well worded summary of Shay's ideas:

> "Shay's thesis on PTSD is that it is **betrayal** that is the core issue. In the military it is betrayal from the top about the mission, in families it is the betrayal of trust in the parent - you can face terrible things,

do them and witness them, if you believe that they are justified. But the void opens up when you know that they are not."

I have noticed similarities between accounts of PTSD and abuse of veterans on the one hand, and accounts of victims of sexual abuse on the other. While there are many obvious differences between mistreatment of veterans and sexual abuse, there is also much psychological overlap because they are both life and death issues that cut to the core of an individual's dignity and self-worth, and they both impact a victim's ability to trust.

An average of 22 or more veteran suicides a day is grave matter.

The effects of service impact the rest of a veteran's life and can be the source of a great sense of accomplishment. But on the flip side, stress can bring you to dark places, personal relationships can become strained or even chaotic beyond the norm, and creating a proper balance in life can be a challenge.

Getting Strong Now

Resiliency is just as important for a military member's life as combat, because of the long-term effects on one's life. The end result can be very negative or very positive.

As far as practical matters concerning veterans, for those that are suffering with PTSD, even if it's undiagnosed, I highly encourage my brothers and sisters to go talk to someone. If in doubt, seek help. Do it anonymously, or talk to someone close to you already – whatever works.

Everyone has their own coping mechanisms. Destroying yourself, either quickly or slowly, is not the way to go. Your life matters in a particularly special way because of your service to our nation – Veterans lives really do matter.

There have been way too many veteran suicides over the past decade and more, way too many. This is another national tragedy. Being strong means opening up to your buddies and speaking about things that you're suffering through.

Adopting a certain mentality can be most helpful. On August 27, 2021, I hosted the Veterans Panel for the Irish Echo's "Big Irish Campfire" in New York City (the Echo is the oldest and most widely-read Irish American newspaper, founded in 1928). There was no literal fire; it was an event held to spotlight our community's activity and vibrancy. The Campfire was another innovative idea turned into reality by my friend Máirtín Ó Muilleoir, who is also the former Lord Mayor of Belfast, Ireland.

This year's event had been in planning for some time, and it had a vibe of specialness; this was the paper's first public event since the start of the COVID pandemic. But an even greater sense of profundity lingered among us because of the previous day's suicide attack in Kabul.

This, and the Afghan withdrawal in general, provided just the right fodder for discussion. We could not have conspired for world events to align with a panel that had been planned months in advance, so it was serendipitous.

One of our panel members was Iraq veteran Brendan Cooney, an Army Reserve Battalion Commander, who had a wise outlook on things. He spoke of the futility of basing the worth of your efforts on things you cannot control, like strategic decisions of the National Security team or the performance of the host nation government. "That's a fool's errand," he said, "I can just base my effort and my immediate effects on what I did. And I'm no less proud of what I did and how I did it." His sense of accomplishment would be maintained whether Iraq or

Afghanistan or wherever were perfect democracies right now or not.

He also gave an analogy that puts things in perspective:

> "So if a doctor treats a patient for 20 years, the patient does well and the patient lives, right? 20 years go by and the patient dies. Has the doctor done any less? Has the doctor wasted his or her time? That person had 20 years to live, make memories, make a family, do good things. The doctor that treated the patient did too. Veterans should know they made a difference."

Adopting such a realistic take on the matter can blunt the force of the trauma. When you know you are not personally responsible for a bad situation, but actually did a lot of good, a wall of psychic separation comes between you and the quislings in power.

Everyone has their own thing for dealing with the enormity of the situation. Greg Papadatos, a superb medic I served with and a Fighting Irish veteran of both Iraq and Afghanistan, said, "I am working a lot lately - many shifts and long shifts. Focusing on work is helping me get through this madness."

He explained that he was using work as one of his coping mechanisms. "Some people don't get that automatically. They see a workaholic, and don't see why that's a good thing at times."

Speaking for myself, the first way that I'm making sense of it is to continue on with the thought process that I already have in place. The end of the war was a long time coming and I've been thinking about these matters for quite some time. I've come to a peace about my own service over there, about the service of my buddies over there – we did our job, we did it well, and it's something to be very proud of.

Going forward, I will continue doing what I'm doing right now: being open, being vocal about these issues that are so important to so many veterans. I speak out, I write. I seek to ensure that our sacrifices are remembered and commemorated, not just in an abstract way, but in a real and present way.

On a spiritual level, I pray.

And in fact, I literally wrote a book on prayer. Calling on heaven is truly essential – the branches cannot survive without the vine. At the end of the day, I have an underlying peace, an existential peace that comes from knowing that God's providence leads everything to its completion, to its proper destiny, and that everything will be all right in the end, ultimately.

But before we get to that point, we have to fulfill our responsibilities in this world. Faithful prayer truly sustains us in that mission.

Rebel With a Cause

I also fight back against sucker punches, and I think this is a healthy mentality for veterans to adopt. For instance, not everybody in America respects military service.

A part of my bomb dog experience demonstrates this. I was a K9 handler with a company called MSA Security for five years. During this time, I had one partner, a beautiful black Lab named Mattie. She worked with me her entire working life and lived at home with my family when she wasn't working. Mattie was approaching retirement when I had to go on military leave to serve my country in uniform again.

At the end of 2018, I informed MSA that I was going to serve on active duty again, but that I would be local and still able to keep up with Mattie's training. Since MSA had previously allowed handlers to keep their dogs in similar circumstances I had no reason to believe this would be different. Except it was. Instead of allowing Mattie to retire with me, or to work out some other arrangement, MSA's CEO Glen Kucera showed what he thought of the honor of military service by abruptly taking her away from my family, her family.

There was no precipitating justification for this. My record was spotless, and MSA themselves called me a "great employee."

But the more I tried to reason with them and work out a compromise, the more belligerent they got – particularly the CEO Kucera, a man with no military or law enforcement experience himself.

Our poor Mattie… Our lovable goofball could not have understood any of this. She must have been wondering how she ended up torn away from her family and everything she knew her whole life. Mattie was just shy of seven years of age and nearing retirement when she was taken in January of 2019.

As of the Fall of Afghanistan in 2021, she was nine and a half years old and still working at an undisclosed location across the country from us. The average lifespan of a Labrador Retriever is 12 years.

But guess what. We *fought back*. I don't mean physically, but with our voices. As of this writing, Mattie is still not home. But through aggressively bringing light to this injustice, we have attracted a tremendous amount of support from elected representatives, media, and regular people. As of the beginning of November, 2021, we have over 261,000 petition signatures on change.org (to learn more, search for "MSA Security: Please return K9 Mattie to her Military Family," and have a look at some further info in the back of this book).

Veterans do not need to be coddled or have some kind of red carpet rolled before them. But at the very least, they should be spared such flagrant *disrespect*. The above experience is not an isolated one concerning MSA; they are known for this. It is evidence that the disrespect of military service, which easily leads to the corrosive thought pattern of defeatism, does not only exist at the upper echelons of government. It is a prevalent cognitive cancer that lurks in the mentalities of elite snobs in all walks of life.

The answer: FIGHT BACK. Even if the end result is the same, your conscience will be clean.

Public Displays of Affection

In terms of public displays, the appreciation shown by American citizens really does make a difference. All the parades, memorial services, and the like, they really do have a positive impact. They wouldn't have lasted for centuries if they didn't serve a purpose. I am not speaking of overloading vets with trite and saccharine sentiments, but genuine and honorable commemorations.

For instance, Charles Sanders is an Army National Guard officer and Afghan vet who gives a stirring presentation in the New York area every single year about the terrorist attacks of September 11. This is an example of a commemorative practice which pays proper and honorable tribute to those who gave everything. Another is my buddy Mark Tolley, whom I served with in the NJ National Guard at the time of the terrorist attacks. He has devoted himself to decorating the bridges of his area of central Jersey with US flags. His group, "Patriotic Bridges of Sewaren/Port Reading" is truly patriotic and honorable.

These public displays are evidence of the genuine regard for military service in the United States, even if such a regard is not universal. If they were done in times past even in memory of victory, they are that much more necessary in this era of defeat from within.

4. ABANDONMENT & BETRAYAL OF ALLIES (a.k.a. Loss of Honor, Repuation)

In terms of the material damage we did to our cause, we have gone over that in Section I. But the deeper issue that lies underneath that is that of honor, reputation, credibility. This is closely related to the previous heading regarding the destructive effect of defeatism.

I have already mentioned that the way veterans are treated by those who send them to war has a profound effect on them, and that frivolously dispensing with the sacrifices of the troops has a distinctly harmful effect on those who served on the front line. Callously disregarding the fate of the Afghan people is one such way of showing flagrant disrespect to *our* troops.

My buddy Chad Paustian was our squad's Dedicated Marksman and a tough, smart, no-nonsense Cavalry Scout. He movingly articulated one of his experiences on our deployment together:

> "I witnessed a little girl have her shoes stolen by a bunch of bullies. I had her bring her father to me. I gave him $20 to get her new shoes. He denied it at first, I believe out of pride, but I explained it was my inaction that let it happen, and since charity is a

pillar of Islam it was my responsibility to fix it. The next time I saw him he invited me to tea, and introduced me to his family, all of whom were wearing new shoes. They live in Ghazni. Ghazni was recently taken over by the Taliban. The Taliban will stone a woman to death for the offense of being raped. And now that family is ruled by them.

This is what haunts me. This is a legacy that I have no control over but desperately wish I could fix…

I made connections on emotional levels with many Afghans. And all for naught…

This is the PTSD that gets overlooked. And the blatant disregard for so many lives that we have left high and dry angers me. I'm angry with everybody that had anything to do with it, and those who support it."

Even if you didn't have a shred of humanity in you, and you just cared about the projection of American foreign policy or you were otherwise just a stone cold type of person, you would recognize the wisdom of sticking by your word.

This notion applies to international relationships as much as it applies to interpersonal relationships. People assess your trustworthiness based on your actions as matched to your words, and deal with you accordingly.

There are those who say that the people of Afghanistan or wherever else can just take care of their own problems. Leave America out of it, let us deal with our own issues at home.

Fair enough – if you mean *before* getting involved.

It becomes very different once you make a real commitment to real people and have ratified that commitment through years of personal involvement. You're stuck with each other now.

It's akin to marriage. If one breaks off a relationship before the wedding day, the hard feelings are comparatively minimal and the parties involved can go their separate ways without too much damage from a mismatched union. But it's a different story if the vows have been exchanged and the union consummated, and especially if it's after the passage of some years and there are children in the picture. In that case, the abandoner is seen by most people (accurately, I believe) as a shameless and contemptible rogue.

If you give a people your word as a nation, that you will stick by them, and that it's worth it for them to stick by you, and for you to be allies and to fight alongside each other, then that would apply even in the case of a Machiavellian giving his word. Even in the case of those who have no real human feelings, no natural human sympathies, they can see the utilitarian benefits of developing bonds of trust with others.

There are numerous soldiers who have been in similar situations where they developed bonds of loyalty with native Afghans. Chad and I are certainly not alone in this, at all, whatsoever.

If we're vocal about it, it's because we're passionate about it, and so are others.

It was Osama bin Laden's grand strategy to provoke America into a quagmire that would leave us humiliated, disgraced, and bankrupt. We squashed those dreams by rapidly driving the Taliban from power in 2001. His hopes then shifted to Iraq, where they seemed to be on the verge of succeeding. However, we eventually got the upper hand there.

But bin Laden is (metaphorically) having a good satanic laugh from beyond the grave, with President Biden's assistance. America was indeed humiliated and disgraced; and not quite bankrupt yet, but heading there.

The disgrace is not just an emotional abstraction; it affects our dealings with the rest of the world. How could other nations ever trust us again, especially for the remaining period of time Biden is in office? A lot of bad stuff can happen in those years.

We the people of the United States made promises. And as I was saying before, even if you were a totally Machiavellian sort of character, you would recognize the value of keeping to your promises, because it affects everything else.

Now I'd like to think that Americans in general are far more than just Machiavellians – that we have human hearts and actually care.

The military expert Donald Vandergriff, who I speak of elsewhere in this book, was against a lasting US presence in Afghanistan. He is on record warning against it back at the beginning of the war, and has expressed that we should have left in December of 2001. And yet, he recognizes that a different approach is required once a commitment has been made, and we are already neck deep in it, and some "modicum of success" has been achieved at considerable sacrifice. He told the *Washington Examiner*:

"How do we know we made a difference? Because if we didn't make a difference, you wouldn't hear about soccer teams fleeing. You wouldn't hear about women's robotic teams fleeing. If there was no real difference… there would be no change. No one would be fleeing."

The Taliban reign of terror has begun. They have not turned over a new leaf, despite the image they are trying to portray (they are similar to North Korea that way). Even in the short time they've been in power, glimpses of the truth have emerged.

My buddy Hekmat Ghawsi, who I mentioned earlier in the context of his heroism in rescuing his wife, and who we'll meet again at the end of Section IV, has this to say:

"There are real videos from across Afghanistan uploaded daily, and shared in private groups across social media, showing that these people [*the Taliban*] are the same animals that they used to be. Their "mercy lists"? They don't have mercy. They're trying to show good faith on PR and stuff like that, just so they can get funding and attention and be accepted in the international community as a legitimate government."

There was one incident that became known at the end of August that struck me as emblematic of the new order. A famous and beloved Afghan folk singer, Fawad Andarabi, was dragged out of his home and executed. The singer's offense was that… he sang. In the Taliban's view, "music is forbidden in Islam." Maybe it's because I'm a Celtic folk singer myself, so I'm particularly horrified, who knows. All I can say is that an assault on music is an assault on humanity itself, and we helped these Taliban monsters come back into power.

Did you know that for centuries Afghanistan had a Christian presence of ancient lineage? St. Thomas and St. Jude Thaddeus are Apostles strongly associated with Afghanistan. Thomas physically preached there, and Thaddeus composed the core of the eucharistic liturgy of the Church of the East, the Anaphora of Addai (Thaddeus) and Mari.

The strong presence continued until the 14th century when the Church was destroyed by the genocidal massacres of Tamerlane. Looking at it now, one would hardly know that Christianity thrived there for so long.

While the overwhelming majority remained Muslim, at least a certain freedom of conscience became regular after the US-led liberation. Perhaps nothing like what is traditional in the States, but at least the organized brutality ended. It is estimated that there are at least 10,000 native Afghan Christians. Not a whole lot in a country of 40 million, but at least they had a chance. Gradually, certain native Afghans felt comfortable enough to openly declare their faith without being murdered. There was a cautious religious toleration, particularly in urban areas.

Now that's all over. Back to the catacombs.

The preventable humanitarian catastrophe is a disgrace to our nation in the eyes of man, and more importantly, I believe, in the eyes of our heavenly Father.

I pray that one day this nation in which so much of America was invested will enjoy the blessings of liberty. But the Afghan people have been set back because of the United States of America betraying our allies, and our own veterans, by *de facto* surrendering to the Taliban.

During my time over there, I asked one of our terps, codenamed "Rambo" – a really great guy – about what it was like during the Taliban's reign of terror. I asked him point blank, "What was it like living under the Taliban before the United States came in and removed them from power?"

I had asked several of them, but his answer really stuck out.

He said, "It was hell."

It was hell. Those are words that stay with me. The reign of terror consisting of the enforcement of an overly strict ideology, its severe punishments for minor infractions, and just the overall misery of the country.

It was *hell*. That's what he said. And all of them agreed. All the other Afghans that I have since spoken to agree with this sentiment, and they all have their own words to express it. But this phrase, *it was hell*, is something that stuck with me. And the hope that we brought to them was that "hell" was going away. They'd have a chance at a good future for themselves and their families.

Hell returned, with the help of senior American leadership.

Even as I write these words, it hurts to know the US let them down. We promised, then reneged. Serpentine dishonor goes directly contrary to my values, so it was not my choice. But it was my country, so it's personally embarrassing.

5. STRENGTHENING OF TERRORISM

2010 was the most violent year of the Afghan War for the US. It was the peak of our combat operations. It was when the most Americans were killed and wounded, and yet despite the violence, there was a cautious sense of hope for the future of Afghanistan. I remember the vibe. There was a sense that our efforts there might result in a country, that even if it was not a fully western-style democratic republic, would at least be modernized to the extent that it would give the Afghan people the best chance for hope. And the major practical benefit that would accrue to the US is that we would deny that land from being used as a base for terrorist operations, which it was prior to 9/11. And sadly, what it is again.

We gave over an entire nation to terrorists. The Taliban is now probably the best armed and best outfitted Jihadist organization in the world, courtesy of the American worker's labor. *That stings.*

I know people were making an argument that once the Taliban takes over, the resulting chaos was not going to bother us. You know, they'll just terrorize their own country.

But that is false; indeed, it is delusionally ignorant. **Al-Qaeda** reigns in triumph along with the Taliban. And **ISIS-K** is making moves to rise to the fore. Let no one be in doubt, the international terrorism that we were supposed to clear out of Afghanistan is now back stronger than ever. And the idea that it can be solved with drones is preposterous beyond description.

Here below is a list of the titles and descriptions of articles on Afghanistan from *FDD's Long War Journal* covering a timespan from the American exit in late August until early November of 2021. Tell me if you don't see the unsettling trend:

> OSAMA BIN LADEN'S SECURITY CHIEF TRIUMPHANTLY RETURNS TO HOMETOWN IN AFGHANISTAN
>
> *Bill Roggio | August 30, 2021*
>
> The video of Dr. Amin al Haq is evidence that Al Qaeda commanders now feel secure enough to appear publicly in a Taliban-controlled Afghanistan.
>
> AL QAEDA PRAISES TALIBAN'S 'HISTORIC VICTORY' IN AFGHANISTAN
>
> *Thomas Joscelyn | August 31, 2021*

Al Qaeda's central media arm, As Sahab, released a two-page statement praising the Taliban's "historic victory" in Afghanistan. Al Qaeda fought alongside the Taliban to resurrect its Islamic Emirate of Afghanistan.

ISLAMIC STATE BOMBS TALIBAN CONVOYS IN EASTERN AFGHANISTAN

Thomas Joscelyn | September 20, 2021

The Islamic State claims to have attacked multiple Taliban personnel and vehicles across the city of Jalalabad on Sept. 18 and 19. [*Note: It's no consolation in this instance that terrorists are killing terrorists. The escalation of hostilities only strengthens Jihadism as a whole – SÓF(F)*].

INFLUENTIAL TALIBAN COMMANDERS APPOINTED TO KEY POSITIONS IN NEW REGIME

Bill Roggio | September 21, 2021

The Taliban appointed former Guantanamo Bay detainee Mullah Abdul Qayyum Zakir as a deputy minister of defense, while Ibrahim Sadr, who has worked closely with Iran in the past, was named a deputy minister of the interior for security.

EX-GUANTÁNAMO DETAINEE PRAISES TALIBAN'S VICTORY, THREATENS AMERICA IN NEW AQAP VIDEO

Thomas Joscelyn | October 6, 2021

Ibrahim al Qosi, a former Guantanamo detainee who worked for Osama bin Laden prior to 9/11, praises the Taliban's victory and threatens new attacks against America in a new video. Al Qosi, who is a senior figure in AQAP, claims that "upcoming operations" may not be a "carbon copy" of 9/11.

MOVEMENT OF THE TALIBAN IN PAKISTAN (TTP) CONSOLIDATES POWER IN TRIBAL AREAS

Bill Roggio | October 7, 2021

With increased muscle, backing and resources, the TTP – which sent thousands of fighters into Afghanistan to help the Afghan Taliban conquer the country over the summer – can now refocus its efforts on its insurgency in order to overthrow the Pakistani state.

EP. 57 — THE EMPEROR WAS NUDE ALL ALONG

WHY EVERY AMERICAN SHOULD BE CONCERNED

Thomas Joscelyn & Bill Roggio | October 14, 2021

Hosts Tom Joscelyn and Bill Roggio discuss Tom's recent testimony before the Senate, why the Islamic State bombed a mosque in Kunduz [*in northern Afghanistan*], and the Pakistani Taliban's ongoing jihad.

TALIBAN APPOINTS KABUL ATTACK NETWORK COMMANDER AS PROVINCIAL GOVERNOR

Bill Roggio | November 9, 2021

Qari Baryal led an element of the Kabul Attack Network, which attacked Coalition and Afghan forces, as well as civilians, in an around Kabul. He is closely allied with Al Qaeda and has received financial support from Iran.

The situation continues to develop and worsen. If you are interested in keeping track of the developments, read everything by *FDD's Long War Journal* (by the way, FDD stands for "Foundation for Defense of Democracies").

And if you are in any doubt as to how international terrorists feel about our disgrace, listen to what Al-Qaeda had to say at the end of August, 2021:

> "We praise the Almighty, the Ominpotent, who humiliated and defeated America, the head of disbelief.
>
> We praise Him for breaking America's back, tarnishing its global reputation and expelling it, disgraced and humiliated, from the Islamic land of Afghanistan."

The Jihadists have been emboldened beyond measure, and far from denying Afghanistan as a base for international terrorists, we are setting them up to be stronger than they ever were, if we do not interrupt them in some substantive way.

And no, not mostly with drones.

Yes, drones can help. But this absurd reliance on them to the expense of deeper solutions strikes me as utterly quixotic. As late as Halloween of 2021, a Reuters article reported that President Biden said the US "will 'respond' to actions Iran has taken against Washington's interests, including drone strikes." *C'mon man*, as lethal as drones may be, I'm about sick of hearing about them as the solution, because they clearly are not.

The President cannot properly execute his duty to "provide for the common defence" with such a one-trick pony show.

Nor, might I add, does the Constitution's mandate to "provide for the common defence" have a 20-year expiration date. Being that we are in a worse position now with regard to Afghan-based terrorism than we were on September 10, 2001, this requires immediate attention by our elected representatives.

We do have one saving grace in this regard: The warm relationships we have built with so many Afghans over the course of two decades, many of whom are now Americans or in the process of becoming Americans. Their efforts to free their native land from a safe base in the Land of the Free could hold the key to protecting America.

Otherwise, the terrorism promoted by President Biden's leadership will continue onto the nightmarish terminus of true dystopia.

6. COMMUNIST CHINA'S PROXY VICTORY

The strongest global competitor of the United States is Communist China, a country that represents oppression, tyranny, government control, and every value that America nominally stands against. Yet, they have reaped a massive windfall from America's humiliation, one that makes them stronger in relation to us and a greater threat to the free world.

One book I highly recommend on the subject of the threat that the Chinese Communist Party (CCP) poses, and which uncovers the details of how China has already been waging a soft war on us, is *Sinoland: The Subversion of Freedom's Bastion* by H. John Poole.

Another necessary work for grasping the problem is *Bully of Asia: Why China's Dream is the New Threat to World Order* by Steven Mosher. The author has a deep encyclopedic knowledge of China's past and present, and we ignore his insight at our peril. I am thankful to him for a conversation in which he pointed out to me that China seeks to "bracket" India. This is of great concern to our security because India is an emerging power and the only country in the world with a population that can match China's. It is also an open democratic nation with values similar to our own. The collapse of Afghanistan has strengthened China in relation to India, especially with the gouging out of the American eye at Bagram.

While China is the big hostile player, Iran and Russia have gotten in on it too. For instance, according to LtCol (Ret) Oliver North, speaking on Sean Hannity's Fox

News show August 30, 2021, the Taliban "is now being helped by Russian GRU officers, intercepting cell phone calls from those begging for help getting out. And what they're doing is they're targeting - that's why you hear those gunshots. They know where to go to find the cell phone, because that person was calling someone in the States in a plea to get out."

These are four major areas in which Communist China is greatly strengthened by the American Afghan debacle, going in order from the most specific and immediate to the most abstract and longest reaching:

A - Reverse engineering of US military technology

B - Gaining access to Afghanistan's untapped mineral riches

C - Boxing in or "bracketing" India, a friend and emerging power

D - Emboldening of aggression, with regard to Taiwan and others

Any one of these is a matter of **vital American national interest**. That all four of these areas are operating in tandem to our detriment is an *absolute scandal*.

Concerning Afghanistan's enormous mineral wealth, one fact not yet commonly known is that much of it was not known publicly before the US-led liberation. Afghan geologists had been keeping it secret out of fear that the Taliban would exploit it. Competent development of mining would have made them the wealthiest terrorists in the world, and thus, the ones having the greatest financial capacity to do damage.

The liberation in 2001 gave the scientists the confidence to come out in the open and share their knowledge, with the safe feeling that comes from knowing that America has your back, the bad guys are gone, and the world will make sure they never come back in power.

And now in 2021, America, under the direction of President Biden, assisted those enemies of civilization to come back into power. Now the Taliban know all about these secret riches that had been kept from them. Now they know, and can partner with the Communists of China to develop these riches for the benefit of evil causes that threaten the American homeland.

Even apart from the need to deny advantage to Jihadist terrorism, America needed to leave Afghanistan from a position of strength and to continue supporting the free Afghan forces, in order to prevent this existential threat from large and hostile foreign powers.

I pray that our elected officials turn their attention to this.

III. HELPFUL ARTICLES

Fritz, Ian. "What I learned while eavesdropping on the Taliban." *The Atlantic*, August 19, 2021.

Hamilton, Katherine. "Report: Taliban killing people found with Bibles on their phones." *Breitbart*, August 17, 2021.

Joscelyn, Thomas. "Al Qaeda praises Taliban's 'historic victory' in Afghanistan." *FDD's Long War Journal*, August 31, 2021.

Klippenstein, Ken, and Sara Sirota. "The Taliban have seized U.S. military biometrics devices." *The Intercept*, August 17, 2021.

Loewenstein, Antony. "Natural resources were supposed to make Afghanistan rich. Here's what's happening to them." *The Nation*, December 14, 2015.

Roggio, Bill. "Osama bin Laden's security chief triumphantly returns to hometown in Afghanistan." *FDD's Long War Journal*, August 30, 2021.

Roy, Siddarthya, and Richard Miniter (Zenger News). "Taliban kill squad hunting down Afghans – using

US biometric data." *New York Post*, August 27, 2021.

Wolman, Jordan. "'There could be still hundreds of Americans' in Afghanistan, former U.S. envoy says." *Politico*, October 24, 2021.

Wright, Robin. "Afghanistan, again, becomes a cradle for jihadism – and Al Qaeda." *The New Yorker*, August 23, 2021.

IV. THOUGHTS ON THE FUTURE – THE SILVER LINING

In terms of the real-life circumstances on the ground in Afghanistan, it looks bleak. It honestly looks very bleak right now. But there is some hope. Maybe not a great hope, but there is *some* hope and you never know what is going to happen in the future – whether there will be a large-scale popular uprising against the Taliban, for instance.

I wrote a well-received book called *Heaven Help Us, Now!* as an act of gratitude to God for some timely blessings I had prayed for and received. The book's subject is St. Jude Thaddeus, the patron saint of hopeless causes (and incidentally, a patron saint of Afghanistan). And this is certainly an appropriate time for the use of prayer to God through St. Jude, because it does seem that Afghanistan is heading in the direction of a hopeless cause.

Scholars will be debating for many years to come about the root causes of the Afghan debacle, and how to avoid getting into similar jams going forward.

At least at the level of what my buddies and I were doing there, we know we did everything to a tee and with the greatest professionalism, to the best of our ability. And we were successful in our lane. Vermont's Green Mountain Boys took to the mountains of Afghanistan with the same freedom-loving spirit that motivated our fighting when we won the Battle of Bennington against England nearly two and a half centuries ago.

But obviously, as this recent war and other recent wars have proven, tactical success in battle does not necessarily equate to overall victory in war. Otherwise, we would not have undergone the recent catastrophe. And like I pointed out above, scholars and academics will be debating this for decades to come.

But we can start working on fixing it right now. I recommend that the following measures be examined and implemented by those with the power to do so:

1) Hold senior military and civilian leadership accountable, including the President himself.

2) Sustain the many good qualities of the US Armed Forces' combat performance, among which are:
    - Never leaving a buddy behind.
    - The best military medical care in the world.

- Exceptional armor and weaponry.

3) Unleash the genius of servicemembers through an organized decentralization known as "Mission Command."

4) Adjust US military operations to account for America's internal weakness due to its political division.

5) Embrace the Afghan American community and support the anti-Taliban freedom movement.

The only real heroism in the Afghan debacle has come from the grassroots, and any success has been from the ground up.

To say that one is a General used to bring with it an automatic sense of awe. It is most unfortunate, but General Officers nowadays are regarded by many veterans with suspicion, as the engineers of humiliation and defeat. In other words, as losers *par excellence*.

Some of them are seen that way anyways, but enough of them and in high enough positions to have a corrosive effect on the fighting ability of the force.

I do believe this is unfortunate, because I, for one, do wish to look to the General Officers of today with the awe and admiration that heroes in their position had earned in times past. And there certainly are some great Generals and Admirals out there, both serving (who I will not mention so as not to draw vengeful scrutiny to them) and retired (around 90 of whom signed the "Open Letter from Retired Generals and Admirals Regarding Afghanistan" calling for GEN Milley's and SecDef Austin's resignation).

The big idea is that it shows how important Commanders are. They can completely obliterate the accomplishments of their subordinates with foolish decision-making. Or, they can lead them to glory by unleashing the collective genius of American servicemembers through wise decision-making.

The importance of competence is just as relevant at the level of civilian leadership, because the Flag Officers themselves answer to civilian authorities; this is the American way. But if the Generals, Admirals, and civilian authorities lead American forces on the path to perdition, it falls on the grassroots to do what they can to salvage the situation.

But what can we do? The disparities in power are great. The lowest private can be dealt the severest punishments for losing a sensitive item such as a rifle or night vision goggles. There is nothing unjust about that, it really is a big deal. But what punishment is in store for the Administration for negligently losing many, *many* sensitive items; indeed, an entire bloody war?

Sure, elections may or may not be one type of consequence. But they only occur at significant intervals of time, they can go either way, and at the end of the day an election is just an election. By all means, concerned citizens should go full force with the electoral mechanisms in place to express the will of the people. But there must be more that can be done.

A person of faith can certainly take comfort in God's providence, and that both mercy and justice will reach perfect fulfillment.

But as far as dealing with the present secular realm, **educating yourself and sharing with your fellow citizens** is the way to go. The greatest punishment that can be imposed on a guilty administration is *truth* reaching a critical mass among a population of free citizens. Only then is true democratic action possible.

I encourage you not to allow yourself to be conned with falsehood and deceit. As far as the specific issue of the betrayal of Afghanistan and America's 9/11 legacy, that's the reason I wrote this book. It is simply a matter of getting justice through the widest possible distribution of truth.

And if that's what we *can* do, then let's do it with all our heart, mind, and soul.

All of us have a voice in this; we are a constitutional republic, in theory. By adopting the wisdom of these measures, the United States can start the long road to recovery from the disaster of the Afghan withdrawal.

Constitutional Crisis in the Military

When a thing ceases to perform the function for which it is designed, by definition it becomes useless. Everything goes out the window regarding it.

As it pertains to military affairs, good order and discipline exist because they are necessary for the military to perform the functions which justify its existence. It would not be able to even try to win wars or battles if there were a generalized breakdown of discipline and consequent disorder in the ranks. In such a case, the Armed Forces would be undermined from the root and the entire reason for its existence would be nullified for as long as such a situation persisted.

Thus, in the interest of the United States, order and discipline is codified, for instance, in the Uniform Code of Military Justice (UCMJ).

What happens though, when it's the leadership, including the Commander in Chief himself, who undermines the institution?

The military's primary purpose is defending our nation by securing victories against enemies in a time of war. It's not simply that this was ignored during the Afghan withdrawal, but that actions were taken counter to this purpose. The very constitutional reason for the military's existence, to "provide for the common defence," was negated.

If you drive a car and your purpose for having the car is your transportation, you have to do potentially unpleasant things such as getting the car registered, getting insurance on it, and doing upkeep and maintenance. This goes on for as long as the car continues to serve the function for you.

But what about a car that no longer works? Let's say the engine is done. The engine is permanently broken beyond repair so it can no longer fulfill its primary purpose for you, transportation. Why would you continue to make other repairs on it, repairs that wouldn't do you any good? Why would you get the tires changed out when the engine doesn't run? Why would you continue to pay insurance on it or keep it registered? No, it needs to be junked.

It's a similar thing in this situation. I say this in the context of Stu Scheller. I read a comment about how its writer had no respect for Scheller because he must have known the UCMJ and its consequences, and he directly violated it. But, I say, **what does UCMJ matter when the President himself *throws a war?***

In LtCol Scheller's Letter of Reprimand, dated October 26, 2021, the Marine Corps' Gen. Alford wrote addressing Scheller, "*You have violated your solemn oath to support and defend the Constitution.*"

And, "*Your actions have harmed good order and discipline with the service as well as publicly discredited the U.S. Marine Corps.*"

And, "*Your narcissistic acts can serve only to erode the rule of law.*"

WHOA.

Those are some accusations. And they're **not** true.

Everything concerning good order and discipline in the military is predicated on the oath each servicemember takes to support and defend the Constitution. This same Constitution designates the President as its supreme defender and as the supreme Commander of the US military. This is the source of authority for the oath of enlistment's stipulation that an enlistee swears to "obey the orders of the President of the United States and the orders of the officers appointed over me, according to regulations and the Uniform Code of Military Justice." The implicit understanding is that all such orders of the President and other officers are lawful, that is, in the support and defense of the Constitution.

But what if the President's orders were unconstitutional, that is, what if they were the most severe degree of "unlawful" – what if he directs the military to violate their oaths by ordering operations that had as their natural and foreseeable consequence the promotion of the war aims of the enemies of the United States?

In such a situation, wouldn't it have harmed good order and discipline and eroded the rule of law *not* to speak up or protest in some manner?

The leadership of the U.S. Marine Corps, as well as that of the rest of the Armed Forces, discredited itself by so unquestioningly being a party to flagrantly unlawful orders from the top. They were unlawful insofar as their *natural and probable consequences* were the *giving of aid and comfort to the enemy* in time of war.

The more surprising thing is what an anomaly LtCol Scheller is. As far as the others on active duty who are secretly sympathetic (and there are many, trust me), I *do* understand the pressure of fearing the loss of your family's livelihood – pay, pension, benefits, the whole enchilada. Financial stability is a powerful motivator for being in outward conformity with the system.

This is not to say that I agree with every detail of every action that Stu Scheller performed. But do I have to in order to in order to agree with his greater cause?

I have read a number of his social media posts in which he shares his opinions on a variety of matters. I agree with him on some, disagree on others. And you know what? That is perfectly okay. *That* is true and legitimate diversity.

The fact is, it is the senior leadership of the United States who violated a clause of the supreme Law of the Land (Article III, Section 3, Clause 1). Stu Scheller's violations of a subordinate code are trifling in comparison, and anything but the very lightest slap on the wrist from the hierarchy will only prove his major point: "My statements all center around the fact that **I do not believe General Officers are held to the same standards as junior leaders.**"

Facts. May God bless him for bringing attention to this, even at the cost of his military career.

So how do we start to correct it?

1) Hold senior military and civilian leadership accountable, including the President himself.

Why did we have to make it easier for the Taliban? Of course, that's a rhetorical question. We didn't have to do that. We should not have done that because it was immoral. The Taliban are evil and unnecessarily cooperating with them is complicity in evil. It is a betrayal of all Americans, and it degrades the dignity of Americans who are asked to give all and who have given all – some 10,000 since 9/11 of 2001.

This is the difference that so many of the senior leadership do not get. If the end result is that the Taliban takes over after our best efforts, our national conscience remains clean. After our *best* efforts. However, acceding to defeatism and systematically demolishing the little "modicum of success" that was bought at such a high price, this is what the betrayal consists of. **It makes all the difference in the world, *even if* the end result is otherwise the same.**

Further, it does not matter if the senior generals and the SecDef did not intend to double-cross their own troops. The totality of their comments give the impression that they believe they did the best they could in difficult circumstances. Perhaps we could all identify with such sentiments; I would never want to be harsher on anybody else than I am on myself. But the results speak for themselves – whether intended or not, they did indeed double-cross their own troops.

Stu Scheller says, and I agree with him, "**Senior leaders accepting accountability would heal more service members than any other initiative.**"

The real test of leadership in upper echelon General Officers for the Afghan withdrawal was the ability to take a stand against the foolish directives of the Administration, even if it meant the loss of a job. Would any of these guys have staked their careers on taking a publicly contrary position to the President?

I was scratching my head for a bit trying to figure out who was most at fault. Based on the testimony of the

Generals who testified on Capitol Hill, the buck truly stopped and started with President Biden.

This is not meant to be a political statement, just a statement of historical fact.

Ultimately, nothing any General would have done would have altered the outcome much because the POTUS was dead set on implementing his ideas.

However, the top brass could have showed courage in confronting such malfeasance. None of them did, least of all GEN Milley.

Accountability might start with the culpable parties saying, "I take responsibility." But that is *only* a start. It must be accompanied by negative consequences for the culpable.

For the sake of the American nation whom they have disgraced, Austin, Milley, McKenzie (and probably others) *must* go.

The subtitle of Andrew Milburn's article on why Secretary Austin should resign is packed with relevance: "Resignation won't atone for lives lost, or the debacle that American involvement in Afghanistan became, but it would at least demonstrate an understanding of professional ethics."

As Father Duffy of blessed memory says, "the loss of rank or position by officers weighs nothing with me in comparison with the two big factors: the proper handling of the men under them; and **victory**."

According to "just war" principles, you have to have a reasonable chance of winning. If we decided that with the American way of war, there was no reasonable chance of overcoming the problems in the DNA of Afghanistan so as to achieve a complete and total victory over the Taliban, okay, fair enough. Then we would withdraw. But at the same time, that does not mean that we roll over and give ourselves up to the enemy in a way that aids the enemy.

You better believe that American Soldiers know what self-sacrifice is about. American Soldiers and other servicemembers have proven with their deeds that they would sacrifice in order to take out the enemy to save their friends. My criticism is about giving up and laying down your superior arms against an evil foe, and then, going even further and putting your head on the block and saying to that foe, "Go ahead. I won't resist you. Decapitate me." This is not "sacrifice" in the sense of a noble and selfless offering of one's own life for the sake of the common good.

The United States surrendered. Perhaps not a surrender *de jure*, but absolutely a surrender *de facto*.

Surrendering is all the more inexcusable because one thing the US can indisputably do well is keep the enemy at bay. We may not have been able to vanquish this particular enemy because the nature of the war does not lend itself to that, but we could have pushed them back. I don't want to say we could have done it with "little effort"; that that makes it seem like it's a walk in the park to pull off. But such operations are the American bread and butter. It's the thing in warfare that we do better than any other nation – you know, "kill people and break things."

In this case, we would be killing the Taliban and breaking them at least in so far as they attempted to take over areas of the country where we were operating to get people out. Only in this manner would we have been able to make a reality of the orderly transition that President Biden said it was going to be.

Instead, we aided the enemy to their victory and our defeat even *before* the war concluded. In the name of over 10,000 dead Americans since 9/11 of 2001, justice needs to be served.

In the old days, kings would be deposed or even executed for leading their people into public shame and disgrace. Ironically, this happened concerning Afghanistan exactly 1,000 years before the US invasion. On November

27, 1001, the Afghan hero Mahmud of Ghazni defeated the Indian army of Jayapala at the Battle of Peshawar. The Hindu ruler survived the battle, but such was the humiliation of defeat that Jayapala executed *himself* by throwing himself into the blazing fire of a funeral pyre.

I'm not suggesting any such result here, that would be un-Christian. But at least this incident shows that there is a certain universality of human emotion in regard to victory and defeat in war. But do these current General Officers have any shame? Does the Administration or President Biden himself have any shame?

I believe they should, because I believe their actions regarding the withdrawal from Afghanistan were criminal. Literally criminal. And they need to be held accountable.

But how could a President possibly be held accountable?

Civilian control of the military is a cornerstone of our Republic, and the President is the Commander in Chief of the Armed Forces. This is clear from the US Constitution. So, isn't everything the President commands with regard to the military legal and binding on servicemembers?

Generally, yes. This is constitutional, thoroughly American, and an overall a good thing. But the Constitution also makes clear that a President is not beyond all reproach.

Undermining the very purpose of your own existence is antithetical to the natural order. A President going against his own country is like the Pope coming out as anti-Catholic, or the Chief Rabbi of Israel coming out as an anti-Semite, or the head of the ASPCA coming out as a torturer of Beagle puppies.

And yet, the Constitution recognizes that such a situation is within the realm of possibility, and further, that it is such a dire situation that special measures are called for to deal with it. The President is mostly immune from prosecution; however, Article II, Section 4, mandates that he, "shall be removed from Office on Impeachment for, and Conviction of, Treason, Bribery, or other high Crimes and Misdemeanors."

We will focus only on the one crime relevant here, which is **treason**.

England had for centuries abused the notion of "treason" and executed untold numbers of people for simply falling afoul of the monarch or his minions. Indeed, the English even extended this false justice into other countries over which they had no right to exercise any authority, such as Ireland, Scotland, and Wales (and India, Kenya, South Africa... the list goes on).

America's Founding Fathers wished to remedy this tyranny and specifically delineated the limits of treason, and codified the legal definition into Article III, Section 3 of the Constitution: "Treason against the United States, shall consist only in levying War against them, or in adhering to their Enemies, giving them Aid and Comfort."

Even with this precise wording, I'd say that most people would need some clarification on what this actually consists of. Some bright light is shed on the subject by Charles Warren's authoritative article from 1918 in *The Yale Law Journal*, aptly titled "What is giving aid and comfort to the enemy?"

There are two distinct branches of treason in the definition. The "levying War" branch does not apply here, because that consists of POTUS assembling an armed force to oppose the United States, which did not happen.

So now we focus on "adhering to their Enemies, giving them Aid and Comfort."

Federal Judge Leavitt, in 1861, delivered an authoritative interpretation: "The words in the definition, *adhering to their enemies,* seem to have no special significance, as the substance is found in the words which follow – giving *them aid and comfort...* In general, when war exists, any act… which, by fair construction, is **directly in furtherance of their hostile designs**, gives them aid and comfort" (the case references are contained in the Warren article).

Even before the adoption of the United States Constitution, the Commonwealth of Pennsylvania expressly defined "the crime of aiding and assisting the enemy" in a 1778 case: "to aid and assist any enemy… by **furnishing such enemies with arms or ammunition, provision, or any other article, or articles, for their aid or comfort, or by carrying on a traitorous correspondence with them.**"

There must be an *overt act*, because the law cannot punish thought crimes. God will punish our willfully evil thoughts, but no mere human rightfully can. Yet, there must also be *intent* to commit the crime. But what does it take to prove intent?

I recall that when I spoke to China expert Steven Mosher at 2021's Catholic Identity Conference, I mentioned to him that, "I don't want to make outright accusations of treason because you don't know what's actually in his mind. But the practical effect of what Biden did is aiding the enemy." This was at an earlier stage of my research into the issue.

As it turns out, doing the deed legally means you intended it. In *United States v. Hodges*, Associate Justice Gabriel Duvall stated, "When the act itself amounts to treason, it involves the intention." Warren explicates: "If, therefore, a person intends to do and actually does specific acts **the natural and probable consequences of which are the giving of aid and comfort to the enemy** [emphasis added], **then he intends to commit treason**, within the purview of the law."

As Warren further explains, "The rule was laid down in *Reynolds v. United States* as follows: 'A criminal intent is generally an element of crime, but **every man is presumed to intend the necessary and legitimate consequences of what he knowingly does**.'" Consequently, a man who commits certain acts, the nature of which are treasonous, is liable to judgement. He does not have to declare, either openly or to himself, "I intend to commit a crime." The act itself demonstrates the intent.

That brings us the next question: *What specific acts are considered to be "giving aid and comfort" to the enemies of the United States?*

Warren lists specific acts that constitute giving aid and comfort to the enemy. Below are those which apply directly to the criminal malfeasance of Afghan withdrawal:

i) Selling goods to or buying goods from the enemy government or to or from its agents or forces.

ii) Communication of intelligence.

iii) Joining the enemy in time of war, or offering service by letter.

iv) Delivering up prisoners and deserters to an enemy is treason.

v) Acts directed against the government or governmental property

with intent to cause injury thereto and in aid of the enemy.

And now, below are *how* these apply to Afghanistan:

A - Providing goods to the enemy government and to its forces (all that abandoned US equipment, and Afghan equipment the US provided and had moral oversight for).

If the President or those under him made the decision to go even beyond selling to the enemy by freely providing goods to them through negligent abandonment, even of those goods under the care of the Afghan National Security Forces which were of US origin and under US moral oversight, this is treason.

B - Communication of intelligence (e.g. Providing Taliban with names and details of Americans and Afghan allies).

If the President or those under him made the decision to communicate to the enemy the identities of American citizens and Afghan allies stranded behind enemy lines, this is treason.

C - Joining the enemy in time of war (e.g. Abandoning Bagram, surrendering Kabul, forcing a premature and rushed exit).

If the President or those under him made the decision to join the enemy by abandoning Bagram Airfield, surrendering the capital city of Kabul, or forcing a premature and rushed exit, this is treason.

D - Delivering up prisoners to the enemy (all those Jihadist prisoners *freely* delivered to the enemy by the abandonment of Bagram Airfield; all those Americans and Afghan allies delivered to the Taliban by abandonment, stemming from the premature and rushed exit).

If the President or those under him made the decision to *freely* deliver all those Jihadist prisoners held at Bagram over to the Taliban – "freely" meaning without getting anything in return in a negotiated settlement, but allowing them to go free out of cowardice or wanton dereliction of duty – this is treason. Further, if the President or those under him made the decision to rush out of the country according to an inflexible deadline with the natural result that American citizens and Afghan allies were left stranded behind enemy lines, this too is treason.

E - "Acts directed against the government or governmental property with intent to cause injury thereto and in aid of the enemy" (the unnecessary destruction, due to the premature and rushed exit, of all the equipment and weaponry meant to fight the enemy, who are now aided by having such equipment and weaponry not being used against them).

If the President or those under him made the decision to destroy the expensive fruits of American labor which were meant to be used by our troops to fight the enemy, thereby aiding the enemy by such destruction, this is treason.

The only people who would possibly be in favor of not following through on the natural and rightful legal conclusion are those who place political gain, or personal power, or the advancement of their own ideologies ahead of the rule of law. The Constitution of the United States is the supreme Law of the Land. It trumps any other human law or political consideration. Anyone who is fair-minded and approaches the subject rationally and objectively, whether Republican, Democrat, or some other affiliation, *anyone who is unbiased* must arrive at the same conclusion.

Only those who place the partisan concerns of a sitting President above justice could possibly be against following the Constitution to its natural outcome. In this kind of grave scenario, it wouldn't matter who was President, or from which political party. If justice is to play out properly, it appears that the impeachment and removal of President Joseph R. Biden is the only recourse under the Constitution.

This would *not* be partisan. Indeed, with Vice President Harris taking the reins, Republicans would gain no political advantage and Democrats would gain another member of their own party in the Presidency, one who would be further to the left than Joe Biden.

This would be a simple matter of **JUSTICE for our nation and for our veterans who fought for it**.

2) **Sustain the many good qualities of the US Armed Forces' combat performance, among which are:**

- **Never leaving a buddy behind.**
- **The best military medical care in the world.**
- **Exceptional armor and weaponry.**

There is so much that the US military does superbly, better than any other military in the world. We should sustain all of it.

The above is a limited list in order just to give the flavor of what I'm talking about. As far as the first, we have already touched on the American military's uncompromising ethic of never leaving a buddy behind. In fact, the violation of that value by our leaders provides a lot of the motivational force behind this book.

This value is so deeply imbued that it takes on the feel of a religious commandment. It is a big reason behind one of the great accomplishments of our forces in these post-9/11 wars, that there are no servicemembers Missing in Action (MIA). As retired Army Lieutenant General Daniel Bolger points out in his encyclopedic *Why We Lost*, our allies took heed:

> "The Iraqi soldiers and police loved the fierce American commitment to recover their dead and wounded, including the Iraqi partners, of course. Saddam's old army had never cared about privates, but Iraq's new army certainly did. It all greatly aided recruitment. Knowing you would come home, dead or alive, meant something in a small village like Diyara."

In addition, the advancement of combat medicine has been unparalleled in human history, and so many of our guys are alive as a result of it. Traditionally in war, there have been two to four wounded servicemembers for every one killed in action. Since the GWOT began, survivability rates for US fighters have skyrocketed. For every American KIA in Iraq, there were *nine* wounded who survived. Even within the GWOT, combat medicine advanced rapidly. For every American KIA in Afghanistan, *eleven* WIA survived (remember, the large-scale Afghan deployments happened after Iraq). Definitely, this is a trend we want to keep going.

The survivability of US servicemembers improved not only because of medical advances, but also through innovations in protective armor. Going forward in tandem with the ever growing lethality and accuracy of US weapons is an ever greater sophistication in our protective equipment.

The development and production of the MRAP (Mine-Resistant Ambush Protected) armored vehicle was one of the greatest life-saving advances in the Global War on Terror, there is no doubt about this. Previously, flat-bottomed HMMWV's (High Mobility, Multi-Purpose Wheeled Vehicles; "Hummers") did not do so well against IEDs (Improvised Explosive Devices). Not even the up-armored ones did well, nor did heavier legacy armored vehicles such as the Bradley Fighting Vehicle or the M1 Abrams tank.

The obliteration of some M1 tanks in the early days of Iraq shocked me when I heard about it. I had grown up in the 1980's thinking that they were invincible because of their highly developed "Chobham" armor, and briefly considered becoming a tanker.

Well, they are pretty darn resilient - if hit from the front. Being thinly armored underneath and flat-bottomed as they are, they will not withstand several hundred pounds of explosives being detonated directly below them.

This is not the case with the MRAP.

"Mayday mayday mayday," is a universally recognized distress call. But my unit actually experienced one particularly severe attack on the literal May Day, in the early fighting season of 2010.

On 1 May, in the Andar district of Ghazni Province, a platoon of our troop went out on a patrol. An IED made of several hundred pounds of HME (Home Made Explosive) detonated directly underneath one of our MRAPs. The 30,000 pound vehicle was blasted straight up into the air and turned forward, landing on its nose, and then tumbled several times before coming to a stop on its side.

A HMMWV, and everyone inside it, would have been disintegrated in the colossal explosion.

Six of my buddies were in that vehicle. They all survived. B Trp 1/172 CAV had many Purple Hearts that day, but all of our guys lived.

One of my buddies, Michael Montgomery, recently quipped when we were reminiscing, "Those trucks were tougher than woodpecker lips."

This is the kind of advancement America needs to sustain.

3) Unleash the genius of servicemembers through an organized decentralization known as "Mission Command."

"Never tell people how to do things. Tell them what to do and they will surprise you with their ingenuity." – General George S. Patton.

We must promote a culture of organized decentralization in order to achieve the best possible results for the common good. A term that encapsulates the underlying principle behind this idea is "subsidiarity." Philosopher Timothy Gordon, taking his cue from Pope Pius XI, lucidly explains in his book *Catholic Republic* that subsidiarity posits that, "it is an injustice and a grave evil and disturbance of right order to assign to a greater and higher association what lesser and subordinate organizations can do."

Subsidiarity is a natural organizing principle that seemingly applies to any complex grouping of humans. Federalism and constitutional liberties are its reflexes in the American socio-political sphere. In the military sphere, subsidiarity takes its form as "Mission Command," which is the loose American translation of the German *Auftragstaktik*.

In layman's terms, this means conducting military missions with simplified rules that guide servicemembers according to their Commander's intent, and which bring the individual initiative of group members into harmony with the overall concept of the operation. Complex and rigid rules are eschewed, and substance triumphs over mere external form.

The foremost authority on this subject is MAJ (Ret) Donald Vandergriff. He is the author of visionary works such as *Adopting Mission Command* and *The Path to Victory* and I highly encourage you to read his work if you wish to gain a better handle on needed reform in the military.

The reason Mission Command is so crucial for recovering from the Afghan debacle is that US forces were hampered throughout the GWOT with the tendency of Commanders to gravitate towards top-down centralization. In addition, one toxic trait of US military culture is an excessive fear of small mistakes, a fear which squelches the boldness required for decisive victory. Also, at the upper echelons there is an excessive reliance on developing tech-based solutions to tactical issues.

Successfully inculcating a culture of Mission Command so that it becomes the universal norm would be a powerful antidote to all these deficiencies.

Back in the 1970's, recently retired Army Lieutenant General Arthur Collins gave a candid and well-respected assessment of US tactical performance in mid-20th century wars. His career lasted from the 1930's to the 70's, a span in which we fought World War II, Korea, and Vietnam. He insightfully noted in his classic book *Common Sense Training* that, "when we went on the offensive, we did not defeat the enemy tactically. We overpowered and overwhelmed our enemies with equipment and fire power."

This is the American way of war heretofore. Inherent in it is the idea, "send bullets not men." This has its blunt force advantages, certainly. But it lacks the tactical finesse required to completely undermine the enemy.

American tactical innovation still manages to bubble into existence wherever we have had to fight. It is a natural thing for humans in mortal danger, such as our servicemembers in combat, to come up with solutions that deal with the situations they are confronted with. Indeed, this trait is perhaps the single greatest survival advantage of our species.

COL (Ret) "Ranger" Mike Malone writes in his classic book *Small Unit Leadership* about one such example of ground-up innovation. He tells of the origin of the "PARFOX" Individual Fighting Position, which utilizes interlocking fields of fire where the deadspace of any one position is covered by the fires of adjacent positions:

> "**PFCs** [*Privates First Class*] **first invented and developed this new fighting position** in our last war [*Vietnam*]. After that war, colonels directed tests and analyses of the effectiveness of the position, and after that, generals made it part of our Army's standard 'how-to-fight' doctrine. **The new position is far more effective** than the fighting position we used before. Effective in terms of *more* enemy and *fewer* friendly killed."

France lost Vietnam because of the battlefield defeat at Dien Bien Phu. The US also eventually lost Vietnam, but not because of a defeat on the battlefield. To the extent that it was allowed, common sense tactical creativity by junior servicemembers deserves a large share of the credit.

And yet, this goldmine of the raw material for decisive victory had to confront the countervailing pressure from above, as described here in Vandergriff's *The Path to Victory*: "Vietnam had become a place to advance one's career as long as officers played it safe, took no risks, became top-down managers, and went along with the use of a doctrine that relied on technology and firepower to fight the war and diminish risk." This ethos still permeates the American military culture, and I can vouch for this with my own experience.

One quick example will suffice. An IED infested road called Route Rattlesnake led directly to my platoon's base, COP Band-e Sardeh. We were all chomping at the bit to take a bat to the hornet's nest and stir things up with the goal of confronting the enemy and destroying him. We did not have to take vehicles; nimble foot patrols would have done the trick. But we were stopped from such aggressive patrolling by Commanders at the Colonel and Brigadier General level, for fear of casualties. Keep in mind that this was in the early stages of the Afghan "surge," when the whole point of the enhanced troop levels was to clear the Taliban out of areas they had retaken.

Our Commander, CPT Doane, was a fighter like us. He reasoned with his bosses, "If you're not going to let us do our job, then what are we doing here? I'm going to send my guys out to find these people." But his bosses absolutely prohibited him from doing so. And thus, we had to use an alternate route out of the COP that did not involve Rattlesnake.

Incidentally, we ended up getting IEDed numerous times anyways. And, thanks be to God, we painstakingly managed to get the overall upper hand over our adversaries and do them some damage. This damage we inflicted included our capture of a highly wanted associate of Osama bin Laden's courier – one small piece of a grand intel jigsaw puzzle that helped lead to bin Laden's killing a year later. But, in this period when the beefed up US presence was supposed to tip the scales decisively in our favor, an opportunity to achieve a truly decisive local victory in our sector was lost because of the Lilliputian mindset of our upper leadership.

This personal anecdote simply describes an instantiation of a wider systemic problem. What was needed during this most intense period of the Afghan War for the US was a truly aggressive surge in which those closest to the reality on the ground had maximum leeway to fight. Ideally, the collective genius of junior servicemembers would have been unleashed by Mission Command in the service of achieving VICTORY IN THE MISSION.

This is what would have given us the greatest chance of doing the most damage to the enemy at the lowest overall cost in casualties to ourselves. *This* kind of combat leadership would have been a genuine testament of appreciation on the part of our leaders for the sacrifices of our troops.

It still might not have won the war, because one of the perpetual issues was the enemy safe havens on the Pakistani side of the border. They could always recoup and recover in the ethnically Pashtun mountains of that region. (By the way, this is another bit of evidence that drones *ain't all dat*, because we droned the living *bleep* out of the Taliban strongholds on the south side of the border for many years. With no boots on the ground to clear them out, they still held on). But it would have **gone a long way to truly annihilating the enemy** insofar as we were able to make contact with him.

Our combat forces continue to preserve and promote outmoded approaches to planning, training, and fighting that have as their origin the rapid wartime military expansion of the industrial age in which a cookie cutter approach was adopted as a matter of efficiency. As Marine veteran and author B.A. Friedman describes in his work *On Tactics* (relevantly subtitled *A Theory of Victory in Battle*):

> "The United States military approach to planning is mechanistic... Adherence to the labyrinth of esoteric rules is ruthlessly enforced, so much so that the process becomes the mission and the mission a tidy but completely useless stack of pages containing the facsimile of a plan. One can become an expert in the byzantine constitution of planning and still be ignorant of planning outside the military, because the labyrinth becomes a prison."

This situation represents the perverse triumph of appearance over substance in American military culture. Compare this to military planning based on the Outcomes Based Learning model of Mission Command. Donald Vandergriff's approach to the planning process is exemplified in this layout of a warning order:

Desired outcomes of a warning order:

1. Subordinates **understand**, and can **explain**, the nature and *purpose* of the upcoming mission.

2. Subordinates **know** *what* preparations they must accomplish for the upcoming mission, *why* they must complete those preparations and *when* those preparations must be complete.

3. Subordinates **have maximum time** to prepare for the upcoming operation.

These operations *do not* restrict the trainee [*or servicemember in a real-world mission*] in terms of methods or techniques that they can use to achieve "success" other than the requirement that they are *appropriate within the context of the current situation and the higher command's intent.*

Those of you with military leadership experience will recognize the stark difference between this and the step-by-step, check-the-box approach that has been the US norm for a good century or so. The approach above requires a mastery of fundamentals and an understanding of the underlying principles. It is geared to emphasize *comprehension* and creative initiative over rote conformity. Mission Command is the military application of the principle of subsidiarity, and as such, its successful implementation can only produce more competent servicemembers, leaders, and results in war.

Universal Application

These principles apply across all walks of life, and the military, political, and corporate spheres can all benefit. Even life at home can benefit.

Individuals having personal agency over their own destinies to the extent that nature and nature's God will allow is simply an inalienable right – a.k.a. "the pursuit of happiness." However, even in practical matters it allows for the greatest chance that things will work out to the greatest benefit for all. As evidence of this, we only need to see the failure and misery brought about by over-centralization everywhere in the world and throughout human history.

Does this mean that all individuals will make all the right choices all of the time? Obviously not, this is absurd. But in aggregate, the sum total of "common good" coming from free individuals acting in accordance with their own reasoning ability will outweigh any good forced down from above.

One of the reasons for this is the cognitive limit imposed by our genetics. Humans have a creativity that no computer can match, as well as massive long-term episodic and procedural memory capabilities. However, none of us are able to hold that many bits of information in our short-term working memory at any given time. This applies just as much to the most intelligent among us, and it applies to Presidents of the United States as well.

There are a staggering number of variables in any given situation in life, and events can spin out of control through a phenomenon known in Chaos Theory as the "butterfly effect." Nobody can truly predict the future. But we can increase our odds of success by gaining a handle on the greatest number of relevant variables in a given situation.

No other human, no matter how smart, could possibly know your life circumstances better than you do. Someone else might have more knowledge in particular subject areas, but nobody has as much of an appreciation of the variables at play in your life as you do.

This matter of fact is applicable to the human population at large. Individuals who have the closest experiential contact with a given situation are those who are actually in it. They might or might not be smart, but it is they who have a more reliable handle on the variables than anybody else.

Beyond the practical matter of *what works*, individuals have the inalienable God-given *right* to determine the best course of action in the situations closest to them. The truth of the principle of subsidiarity plays out with astonishing universality across multiple domains: religious, political, and military.

In history, the highly centralized Roman Empire was eventually defeated by barbarians with looser command structures. (On the other hand, the earlier centralized, but not overly centralized, "Mission Commanded" Roman army under Julius Caesar defeated the kaleidoscope of individual Gallic tribes). The highly centralized Chinese Empire certainly achieved a lot in the days of old, but was eventually surpassed by the patchwork of European states, each competing against each other and developing innovations in accordance with that competitive drive.

Incidentally, one does not need to delve too deeply to make contact with the downside of the Old European competition - colonialism, brutality, oppression, slaughter. My own ancestors were victims of a diabolical English expansionism. But these evils are a result of evil itself infecting the human race, and not of a lack of central authority. Indeed, totalitarian centralizing regimes are guilty of at least as much evil, and in their case, oppression is actually built into the system itself.

Upward Power, Downward Spiral

And yet, top-down centralizing tendencies tend to accumulate hubris. Donald Vandergriff has written insightfully about a "zero-defect" culture of fear of making even tiny mistakes, so that only the sheepish and politically compliant make it to the top. I've seen this with my own eyes, I know many of you with military experience have too.

The pattern repeats itself so many times over. Someone at a lower level will mess up and it will be seen publicly and "go viral," causing embarrassment to superiors. Superiors are asked questions by suspicious or critical observers - reporters, the public, elected officials, whoever. The superiors respond by implementing measures that restrict subordinates in some way, taking just that much more freedom and discretion away. Just a dab, just an increment.

The subordinates' psychological response is to become that much more fearful of making a mistake in the eyes of their superiors. One common result is that they often come down that much harder on their own subordinates. Just a dab, just an increment.

This pattern is seen in many walks of life, including the corporate and the political. Mental discipline is required to understand the true benefits of organized decentralization based on the principle of subsidiarity. Otherwise, we will continuously fall into this loop, this spiral down the toilet. The result is men like Milley, Austin, and McKenzie.

4) Adjust US military operations to account for America's internal weakness due to its political division

As painful as it is to admit for those who treasure the Union, America is so sharply divided that if this were another time and place, a violent shooting war could have conceivably erupted. Let us praise the LORD that this is not the case. Yet, it remains clear that the nation is divided sharply into fervently and diametrically opposed camps that expound incompatible views on the very nature of the Republic. This is not to say that every citizen falls easily within either camp, but there are two discernable centers of socio-political gravity.

Fundamentally, the two centers of gravity differ in their ideologies concerning attachment to and veneration for the natural freedoms ("unalienable Rights") encoded in the very charters of our existence, our "national DNA," so to speak: the Declaration of Independence and the Constitution.

This severe fissure in the body politic of our nation has a fundamental relevance for matters of war and peace. Even if, hypothetically, the US could sustain multi-year wars that go on indefinitely without the terrible results we've seen, the country is too split politically to make it happen – it is "rent in twain" as archaic language would put it. Any overseas operations need to take this into account.

"What about Trump?"

While this book focuses on the events in the middle of 2021, during which time Joe Biden was President, I feel I must address this question because it is a recurring one I keep hearing and getting from certain quarters. It's a peculiar phenomenon I've seen expressed in certain people, to want to pin any and every problem in America on him.

My answer is really quite simple.

IF President Trump had withdrawn from Afghanistan in the disgraceful manner that President

Biden did, I would be just as strong in my negative appraisal of him as I am of Biden.

But he didn't.

In fact, all the available evidence of his documented foreign policy indicates that he would not have allowed such a catastrophe as actually happened. He did not take being bullied by anybody, at home or abroad. President Trump was no interventionist, by any means. But he did vigorously deal with violent threats. Notably, he finished off the Islamic State's territorial hegemony in the Middle East and took out Iran's terrorist in chief, Major General Qassim Soleimani.

The challenge was that President Trump's plan to withdraw our forces from Afghanistan could only have worked successfully if he had had a second consecutive term in office. In such a case, the force of his personality and the fear our enemies had of him would have ensured that nothing of what we saw in the summer of 2021 would have happened.

The problem is twofold.

One, he didn't get a second consecutive term. In Biden's hands, the withdrawal collapsed into the humiliating disgrace that is the subject of this book.

Two, Trump's personal leadership could only go so far even in a best case scenario – eventually, he would have to leave the Commander-in-Chiefship in the hands of a successor.

What I said on this subject in my 2020 conversation with J.P. Lawrence of the *Stars and Stripes* deserves being printed again here:

> The worrisome part is that American policy changes when administrations change, leaving the sacrifices of our servicemembers at the mercy of people with differing foreign and defense attitudes and policies.
>
> In Vietnam, a similar peace deal was made [*as that for Afghanistan*]. And we promised to have South Vietnam's back if the North were to do anything again. The US administration changed, the North invaded, and Vietnam was lost.
>
> We can prevent a similar thing from happening again. But history worries me, as does **the fickleness of US political cycles.**

Soldiers and other servicemembers are pleased to be of service to their country and are typically pleased to fight –

as long as their sacrifices are not in vain. It's actually pretty simple.

Perhaps the military operations we should focus on are shorter, but highly violent and punishing punitive expeditions. Get in, destroy the enemy, get out. Wash, rinse, repeat as many times as necessary for our national security.

Perhaps military and policy planners should envision a four-year cap for any longer foreign interventions. We are not talking about circumventing the natural course of a war through declaring its artificial end by fiat. It's just that it's irresponsible to devise grand strategy without realistically taking into account its sustainability, a sustainability that is undermined by the disease of fundamental division that eats at the root of our nation.

5) Embrace the Afghan American community and support the anti-Taliban freedom movement.

The Afghan American community has much of value to contribute to the United States. Our country has gained incredible strength from those who fled to America to gain freedom from oppression. The Vietnamese who fled to America and contributed so much good to their new nation were one the bright spots in an otherwise tragic period. The Irish are also among those who fled and built something glorious in their new home; I'll say a few words on this because I know this matter well, and it can serve as a model for the Afghan community.

The Irish immigrant community organized in the United States to support freedom from British tyranny for the land of their birth and origin, but they also became fully and thoroughly American.

One of their great contributions to the American heritage is the Gaelic warrior spirit. For instance, the "Fighting" 69th Infantry Regiment of the New York National Guard is one of the shining legacies of the Irish community to this nation. In the wake of the failed 1848 Rising in Ireland, which erupted in the wake of a genocidal famine, the leaders fled to the States and regrouped in New York. They founded what became the 69th as an Irish Republican militia. However, the Regiment ended up providing its greatest service to its new nation – the 69th has fought in most of America's wars since their 1849 founding, "From Bull Run to Baghdad" and beyond.

In fact, as then Captain (and now Colonel) Sean Flynn noted in his book *The Fighting 69th: From Ground Zero to Baghdad*, "The U.S. Army relied on the Fighting

69th so heavily in the late nineteenth and early twentieth centuries that the regiment had earned more battle credits than any other in the world except the Black Watch out of Scotland." No wonder MacArthur told them, "You have written your own history and have written it in red on your enemies' breast."

The natural Irish love of freedom and hatred of oppression directly led to outstanding contributions which benefitted all citizens of the United States. The Irish in America, both immigrants and descendants, also contributed in decisive ways to the cause of Irish independence from the mid-19th century onward. The Afghans who become Americans can similarly make great contributions to their adopted nation, at the same time as they support Afghan liberty.

The diverse Afghan cultures display many common traits that can only bolster the better angels of America's heritage, such as their high regard for family, loyalty, and morality. And, Afghan cuisine, properly cooked, is delicious!

Afghan American communities have started to form groups and fraternal organizations dedicated to integrating newcomers into the community of American citizens, while simultaneously advocating for causes that promote the freedom of their homeland.

One such group is the Freedom Support Alliance (FSA), run by my friend, Hekmat Ghawsi. He is leading this nonprofit organization which he calls, "the biggest project of my lifetime… Veterans, Interpreters, Experts and community members have been working on this project for over 2 years now." In my eyes, Hekmat is clearly imbued with the spirit of Massoud, the Afghan National Hero.

FSA's level of activity has shot up exponentially since the withdrawal, and consequently, so has their need for funding. I encourage you to read about them here:

"FREEDOM SUPPORT ALLIANCE

Our purpose is to honor, support, and advocate on behalf of military interpreters and their families.

YOUR SUPPORT MAKES FREEDOM POSSIBLE

FSA's **goal** is to promote the overall well-being of wartime allies by providing support, hope and a system designed to provide financial independence. After years of service and sacrifice, military interpreters have risked not only their lives but also the lives of their families to defend American freedom.

FSA works to create a diverse and empowered support system to honor the service of U.S. allies and military interpreters. Advocate on behalf of military interpreters, their families, and those who served alongside the United States Armed Forces engaged in the global war on terror.

Whom it serves: Wartime allies, military interpreters, their families and Special Immigration Visa (SIV) recipients.

How it serves: Provide relief services, humanitarian aid, and partnerships with community resources and service organizations interpreters, war time Allies and their families who are facing life-threatening situations Our **Focus**:

We help children, families, and communities of war time allies break the cycle of poverty by empowering people of all ages to dream, aspire and achieve.

Our PROGRAMS:

· Resettlement Services

· Community Resources

· Financial Mentoring

· Cultural Integration

· Advocacy"

Their website is www.freedomsupportalliance.org. These guys do tireless work and are a source of real hope.

With a secure base in the Land of the Free and the Home of the Brave, the Afghan expats can support the anti-Taliban pro-freedom movement in their native land. The organized movement is known as National Resistance Front of Afghanistan (NRF). The American Irish can provide a good model; with a decent measure of success they politically supported, funded, and armed the cause of Irish freedom over a long period.

The American Afghans can do this through political pressure on US elected officials. They can do it through financial support of freedom; greater monetary resources are still an advantage that those based in America collectively have over hostile forces abroad (the Taliban are not rich – yet).

And, with the cooperation of the US government, they can help with the provision of arms and other material warfighting resources to the fledgling resistance, which is currently holding the Panjshir Valley against the Taliban. We helped the Afghan people in such a manner in their struggle for liberty against Soviet Communist oppression. We can do it again to help them in their struggle for liberty against the oppression of the Islamist Jihadist Taliban and their Chinese Communist allies.

The burgeoning Afghan American community is a bright shining ray of hope. It shimmers off the reflection from the silver lining in the dark cloud of the Fall of Afghanistan.

By implementing the measures introduced here in Section IV, and by having a robust public discussion on further improvements needed to recover, we can start to undo the severe damage to our beloved American nation caused by the betrayal of Afghanistan and America's 9/11 legacy.

GOD BLESS AMERICA

IV. HELPFUL ARTICLES

Clark, James. "Marine Commander relieved over viral video calling out military leaders for Afghanistan withdrawal." *Task and Purpose*, (updated) August 30, 2021.

Coontz, Lauren. "The Green Beret who knew how to win Afghanistan." *Coffee or Die Magazine*, August 18, 2021.

Fratus, Matt. "Remembering Afghanistan's national hero, Ahmad Shah Massoud, the 'Lion of Panjshir.'" *Coffee or Die Magazine*, August 31, 2021.

Friedman, B.A. "The End of the Fighting General." *Foreign Policy*, September 12, 2018.

Gordon, Timothy J. "Only Subsidiarity Can Save the Republic." *Crisis Magazine*, October 12, 2021.

Joyce, Kirsten. "Former US Special Forces interpreter works to rescue wife in Afghanistan." *KLAS CBS8 News Now, Las Vegas*, (updated) August 17, 2021.

"Open Letter from Retired Generals and Admirals Regarding Afghanistan." (Flag Officers 4 America). August 30, 2021.

Passoth, Kim. "Las Vegas rideshare driver helps facilitate wife's escape from Afghanistan." *KVVU Fox 5, Las Vegas*, August 25, 2021.

Pullman, Joy. "Mark Milley deserves to be fired and court-martialed for his Afghanistan lies." *The Federalist*, August 18, 2021.

Reynolds, Glenn H. "US troops' rage at their leaders will grow unless there's deep reform." *New York Post*, September 7, 2021.

Rosenberg, Rebecca. "Marine officer blasts major general for calling him 'narcissistic' in reprimand letter." *Fox News*, November 1, 2021

Todd, David M. "Review: Adopting Mission Command: Developing Leaders for a Superior Command Culture by Donald Vandergriff." *The U.S. Army War College Quarterly: Parameters*, 51(3), Autumn, 2021.

Van Brugen, Isabel. "US Marine resigns, seeking accountability from military leaders over Afghanistan withdrawal." *The Epoch Times*, August 30, 2021.

Warren, Charles. "What is giving aid and comfort to the enemy?" *The Yale Law Journal*, 27(3), January, 1918.

Woodruff, William A. "If junior officers had botched Afghanistan, they'd all be fired right now." *The Federalist*, September 13, 2021.

POSTSCRIPT

The particular Afghan War that began on 9/11 of 2001 is now over. But there is every reason to cultivate hope. The fight against evil never ceases, and the good guys do score victories.

My conscience compelled me to write this book. *The Pullout Sellout* has been a follow up to the interviews I gave in a variety of national and international media outlets during the Fall of Afghanistan. There was just more to be said beyond what those interviews had the time for. For instance, I recorded a half hour for CNN's Erin Burnett back in August, 2021. None of it aired.

There is nothing unusual about this in the media world; it's nothing personal (and they treated me wonderfully and with respect). But the interview that never aired did spur me to start writing this. I felt strongly, in the depths of my heart and soul, that there were things that needed to be said. And they weren't said, even at the height of the media attention.

I also knew what skillful politicians like President Biden take advantage of, that public memory is fleeting and that the anger *du jour* would drift into abeyance. To

APPENDIX A – SUMMARY

whatever extent my one-in-330 million voice will allow, my conscience cannot let this drop. I am determined not to let this issue be forgotten; the service of our veterans and our very nation is at stake.

In the deep interior of my soul, I carry the most profound existential peace. This is the case no matter whatever crazy personal trial or suffering I might be going through – it functions in bad times as well as in good. It is difficult to describe the subjective experience of it, but it suffices to explain that it derives from the certain knowledge that God will triumph in *everything*, and that His triumph is ours if we join ourselves to Him.

Indeed, I wrote a previous book about prayer, and the supernatural side of things should not be forgotten. While *The Pullout Sellout* is not expressly religious, I would be remiss if I didn't at least give some account for what might be taken by some as senseless optimism.

Faith is a very real thing to me. If you have faith, you understand that God operates on His level, which is beyond all human comprehension. But He's also very intimately bound up with what we do here, because He is the lover of mankind.

We live here in the world right now, and we have to do things here on earth, in the sphere in which we exist.

One summer night in July of 2010, I was at COP Charkh in Logar Province painfully hobbling on a newly broken ankle. We had been out in some very hostile territory for a couple of days with no vehicles. Somehow, I managed to walk (excruciatingly!) to the nearest base with my platoon, but now I was out for the count. They went out on mission again.

I had to watch the ensuing battle from afar. It was raging only a few "clicks" away. My platoon and a sister platoon had been surrounded and attacked by a large Taliban force from the Haqqani Network. It was perhaps the most terrible and beautiful series of sights and sounds I had ever been exposed to – the explosions, the choppers attacking and devastating the Jihadists, the gunfire from weapons of diverse types and calibers, merrily making their staccato music as our side threw everything at the enemy to keep them from overrunning us.

It was frustrating. I was chomping at the bit for several hours, dying to get out with my brothers.

Long story short, we won – the enemy was slaughtered. Our guys flew back to the COP to get the guys left behind. I loaded onto the chopper for the ride back to our home base in a different province.

Everyone was worn, dirty, with shredded clothes. My comrades helped me into a seat on the bird. The faces were serious, stern… and joyful. We *won*.

My buddy Gary Keefer was right next to me.

"You missed it," he said with a solemn smile.

I confidently replied, "There will be other fights."

I was bummed that I missed this fight, no doubt about it. But I was certain my reply was correct.

And it was.

These fights are not necessarily all in the area of physical combat, but in the war between good and evil that we all have been drafted to serve in. The *Catechism of the Catholic Church* (paragraph 409) tells us this poignant lesson:

> "This dramatic situation of 'the whole world [which] is in the power of the evil one' makes man's life a battle: The whole of man's history has been the story of dour combat with the powers of evil, stretching, so our Lord tells us, from the very dawn of history until the last day."

The battle flag of the US Army's Civil War Irish Brigade, of which the "Fighting" 69th of New York was the core unit, has an Irish motto across it that expresses the spirit these Gaelic warriors brought to the American Republic, a spirit that has energized my own endeavors here: *Riamh Nár Dhruid Ó Spairn Lann*, "Who Never Retreated From the Clash of Spears."

I consider the writing and publishing of *The Pullout Sellout: The Betrayal of Afghanistan and America's 9/11 Legacy* to be as important a service to our great nation as anything I ever did in the military. It was to honor my brothers in arms that I wrote it, and its initial release on Veterans Day, 2021, was geared to that end.

There's more in the cue. We fight on.

My basic principles are based on Christ's Sermon on the Mount. And so, I close with an earnest prayer from my faith tradition: May Christ our True God have mercy on us and save us through the prayers of His all-pure Mother, of our Father among the saints John Chrysostom, Archbishop of Constantinople, and of all the saints, for He is good and loves mankind. AMEN.

APPENDIX A

SUMMARY

WHAT HAPPENED

In Afghanistan during the summer of 2021, the United States forces under the command of President Joseph R. Biden, Secretary of Defense Lloyd Austin, Chairman of the Joint Chiefs of Staff General Mark A. Milley, and the Commander of the United States Central Command General Kenneth F. McKenzie, Jr., disgraced the United States and its 9/11 legacy by the misdeeds listed below. They:

1) Removed assets from Afghan forces (air, intel, logistical, etc.) which we had trained them to depend on for fighting – and then blamed the Afghans for not fighting!

2) Abandoned Bagram Airfield (the only strategic air base in the country) with great combat speed and efficiency, and without coordinating with the Afghan relief.

3) Voluntarily gave up – yes, *surrendered* – the capital city of Kabul to the Taliban - even when the enemy had offered not to contest American control.

4) Gave the Taliban the names of American civilians in the country and of Afghans who supported us.

5) Refused to allow US troops to leave the confines of Kabul Airport to conduct rescues.

A – Americans and Afghan friends were thus left to make it to the airport on their own, and at the mercy of the Taliban.

B – Thousands of US and allied troops were jam packed into a relatively small area to be sitting ducks for attacks.

C – When troops and civilians were inevitably killed, the US leadership retaliated with a deliberate precision strike that did not kill a single terrorist, but did kill several little children.

6) Ignored the counsel of allies in order to rush out of the country according to the timeline the Taliban ordered the US to follow.

7) Gave the Taliban unprecedented leverage over the US and others through negligent abandonment of:

APPENDIX A – SUMMARY

A - American citizens.

B - Afghan allies.

C - contract work dogs and rescue dogs.

D - many billions of dollars worth of lethal and "sensitive item" arms and equipment.

WHY IT'S SO BAD

1) Ignorance of the fundamental need for victory.

2) Failure to understand the enemy.

3) Destructive effect of defeatism on veterans and families.

4) Abandonment and betrayal of allies (a.k.a. Loss of honor, reputation).

5) Strengthening of terrorism.

6) Communist China's proxy victory, through:

A - Reverse engineering of US military technology

B - Gaining access to Afghanistan's untapped mineral riches

C - Boxing in or "bracketing" India, a friend and emerging power

D - Emboldening of aggression, with regard to Taiwan and others

HOW CAN WE START TO FIX IT

1) Hold senior military and civilian leadership accountable, including the President himself. **Treason** was committed by giving **aid and comfort to the enemy** through:

A - Providing goods to the enemy government and to its forces (all that abandoned US equipment, and Afghan equipment the US provided and had moral oversight for).

B - Communication of intelligence (e.g. Providing Taliban with names and details of Americans and Afghan allies).

C - Joining the enemy in time of war (e.g. Abandoning Bagram, surrendering Kabul, forcing a premature and rushed exit).

D - Delivering up prisoners to the enemy (all those Jihadist prisoners *freely* delivered to the enemy by the abandonment of Bagram Airfield; all those Americans and Afghan allies delivered to the Taliban by abandonment, stemming from the premature and rushed exit).

APPENDIX A – SUMMARY

E - "Acts directed against the government or governmental property with intent to cause injury thereto and in aid of the enemy" (the unnecessary destruction, due to the premature and rushed exit, of all the equipment and weaponry meant to fight the enemy, who are now aided by having such equipment and weaponry not being used against them).

2) Sustain the many good qualities of the US Armed Forces' combat performance, among which are:

- Never leaving a buddy behind.
- The best military medical care in the world.
- Exceptional armor and weaponry.

3) Unleash the genius of servicemembers through an organized decentralization known as "Mission Command."

4) Adjust US military operations to account for America's internal weakness due to its political division.

5) Embrace the Afghan American community and support the anti-Taliban freedom movement.

APPENDIX B

General Douglas MacArthur's speech to the 165th Infantry (69th Regiment New York National Guard) on the eve of America's entry into the Second World War

No greater fighting regiment has ever existed than the One Hundred and Sixty-fifth Infantry of the Rainbow Division, formed from the old Sixty-ninth Regiment of New York. I cannot tell you how real and how sincere a pleasure I feel tonight in once more addressing the members of that famous unit. You need no eulogy from me or from any other man. You have written your own history and have written it in red on your enemies' breast, but when I think of your patience under adversity, your courage under fire, and your modesty in victory, I am filled with an emotion of admiration I cannot express. You have carved your own statue upon the hearts of your people, you have built your own monument in the memory of your compatriots.

One of the most outstanding characteristics of the regiment was its deep sense of religious responsibility, inculcated by one of my most beloved friends – Father Duffy. He gave you a code that embraces the highest moral laws, that will

APPENDIX B – MACARTHUR'S SPEECH TO THE FIGHTING 69TH

stand the test of any ethics or philosophy ever promulgated for the uplift of man. Its requirements are for the things that are right and its restraints are from the things that are wrong. The soldier, above all men, is required to perform the highest act of religious teaching – sacrifice. However horrible the results of war may be, the soldier who is called upon to offer and perchance to give his life for his country is the noblest development of mankind. No physical courage and no brute instincts can take the place of the divine annunciation and spiritual uplift which alone will sustain him. Father Duffy, on those bloody fields of France we all remember so well, taught the men of your regiment how to die that a nation might live – how to die unquestioning and uncomplaining, with faith in their hearts and the hope on their lips that we might go on to **victory**.

Somewhere in your banquet hall tonight his noble spirit looks down to bless and guide you young soldiers on the narrow path marked by West Point's famous motto – duty, honor, country.

We all hope that war will come to us no more.

But if its red stream again engulfs us, I want you to know that if my flag flies again, I shall hope to have you once more with me, once more to form the brilliant hues of what is lovingly, reverently called by men at arms, the Rainbow.

May God be with you all until we meet again.

SELECT BIBLIOGRAPHY

Bolger, Daniel. *Why We Lost*. Mariner Books, 2015.

Buckley, James L. *If Men Were Angels: A View From the Senate*. Putnam, 1975.

Catechism of the Catholic Church. Libreria Editice Vaticana, 1994.

Collins, Arthur S. *Common Sense Training: A Working Philosophy for Leaders*. Presidio Press, 2nd Edition, 1998.

Duffy, Francis P. *Father Duffy's Story: A Tale of Humor and Heroism, of Life and Death with the Fighting Sixty-Ninth*. George H. Doran Company, 1919.

Entezar, Ehsan M. *Afghanistan 101: Understanding Afghan Culture*. Xlibris, 2008.

Flynn, Sean Michael. *The Fighting 69th: From Ground Zero to Baghdad*. Penguin Books, 2008.

Friedman, B.A. *On Tactics: A Theory of Victory in Battle*. Naval Institute Press, 2018.

Gordon, Timothy. *Catholic Republic: Why America Will Perish Without Rome*. Crisis Publications, 2019.

Grossman, Dave. *On Killing: The Psychological Cost of Learning to Kill in War and Society*. Back Bay Books, 2009.

Levin, Mark R. *Ameritopia: The Unmaking of America*. Threshold Editions, 2012.

Malone, Dandridge M. *Small Unit Leadership: A Commonsense Approach*. Presidio Press, 1983.

Marlin, George J. *Christian Persecutions in the Middle East: A 21st Century Tragedy*. St. Augustine's Press, 2015.

Milburn, Andrew. *When the Tempest Gathers: From Mogadishu to the Fight Against ISIS, a Marine Special Operations Commander at War*. Pen and Sword Military, 2020.

Mosher, Steven W. *Bully of Asia: Why China's Dream is the New Threat to World Order*. Regnery Publishing, 2017.

Ó Fianghusa (Fennessy), Séamus. *Heaven Help Us, Now!: A Self Help Guide to God's Own First Responder, St. Jude Thaddeus*. Im Úr Blasta, 2021.

Peters, Ralph. *Never Quit the Fight*. Stackpole Books, 2008.

SELECT BIBLIOGRAPHY

Poole, H. John. *Peleliu Progress*. Posterity Press, 2021.

---. *The Iwo Alamo*. Posterity Press, 2020.

---. *Sinoland: The Subversion of Freedom's Bastion*. Posterity Press, 2016.

---. *One More Bridge to Cross: Lowering the Cost of War*. Posterity Press, 2003.

Shay, Jonathan. *Odysseus in America: Combat Trauma and the Trials of Homecoming*. Scribner, 2003.

---. *Achilles in Vietnam: Combat Trauma and the Undoing of Character*. Simon & Schuster, 1995.

Squires, Andrew. *Chasing The Taliban: One Soldier's Memoir of Afghanistan*. CreateSpace, 2018.

Vandergriff, Donald E. *Adopting Mission Command: Developing Leaders for a Superior Command Culture*. Naval Institute Press, 2019.

---. *The Path to Victory: America's Army and the Revolution in Human Affairs*. Presidio Press, 2002.

MORE INFO: IM ÚR BLASTA

CREIDEAMH, CANAMHAIN, agus COGADH.

Im Úr Blasta, LLC (founded October 7th, 2020) is the exclusive publisher for the works of Séamus Ó Fianghusa (Fennessy): Bestselling Author, Combat Veteran, Celtic Revivalist.

Writing on FAITH, FRANKNESS, and FENIANISM.

To learn more, please visit www.imurblasta.com

Feel free to check out our Facebook pages:

Séamus Ó Fianghusa /Fennessy/
https://www.facebook.com/ImUrBlasta

St. Jude: Heaven's 9-1-1 (Public page)
https://www.facebook.com/heavenhelpusnow/

St. Jude: Heaven's 9-1-1 (Private prayer group. Free, simple, and easy to request membership)
https://m.facebook.com/groups/460929235194215/

TITLES FROM *IM ÚR BLASTA*:

Heaven Help Us, Now!: *A Self Help Guide to God's Own First Responder, St. Jude Thaddeus.*

The Pullout Sellout: *The Betrayal of Afghanistan and America's 9/11 Legacy.*

UPCOMING TITLES FROM *IM ÚR BLASTA*
(In probable chronological order):

America's Sweetheart, K9 Mattie

A Brief Introduction to the Fighting 69th

Separation of Church and Virus

Gaelic Warrior

Agus teidil le theacht amach i nGaeilg fosta, ar ndóigh:

Tabhair Cú9 Meaití Abhaile

Gaiscíoch Gaelach

... agus tuilleadh!

Just a note: God will triumph in *everything*, and His triumph is ours if we join ourselves to Him. As He assures us through His prophet Obadiah (vv. 21, 15 RSV), "Saviors [*victorious Israelites*] shall go up to Mount Zion / to rule Mount Esau; / and the kingdom shall be the LORD's… For the day of the LORD is near upon all nations. / As you have done, it shall be done to you, / your deeds shall return on your own head."

MORE INFO: BRING K9 MATTIE HOME

Please see our petition to bring our dog home on change.org:

MSA SECURITY: PLEASE RETURN K9 MATTIE TO HER MILITARY FAMILY

K9 Mattie served with served with me her entire working life and was approaching retirement when I had to go on military leave to serve my country in uniform again. Instead of allowing Mattie to retire with me, the private contractor showed what they thought of the honor of military service by tearing her from us and moving her across the country to keep her away from my grieving family. The following is the petition letter, written by my wife Deirdre.

"I have tried to sit down to write this message several times but have failed as my family and I have been overcome with tremendous sorrow.

My husband, combat veteran SSG Séamus Fennessy was a K9 handler with MSA Security for five years. (UPDATE: MSA Security is now owned by Allied Universal, as of September, 2021). During this time Seamus and his K9 partner Mattie worked exclusively with each other - Mattie never had another handler nor had Seamus had another dog. At the end of 2018 my husband informed MSA that he was going to serve his country on active military duty but would be local and still able to keep up with Mattie's training. Since MSA had previously allowed handlers to keep their dogs in similar circumstances we had no reason to believe this would be different. Except it was. At the 11th hour only 2 days before my husband went on orders we were abruptly informed that Mattie would need to be returned and someone "would pick her up in the morning".

Mattie was just shy of 7 years of age and nearing retirement when she was taken in January of 2019. Upon her birthday, April 26th, 2022, she will be 10 years old; she is currently still working, far away from home. The average lifespan of a Labrador Retriever is 12 years.

MSA CEO Glen Kucera has callously torn our family member, our beloved "Mattie Cakes," from her family who loves and adores her. While our daughters and myself could hardly contain our tears, my husband remained strong despite a barrage of phone calls and texts from MSA which included threats of destroying his military career.

My husband is a decorated combat veteran – and in the words of MSA themselves a "great employee." Mattie is a goofy, lovable pooch who adores playing with the kids in our backyard and napping on the sofa. Neither deserve this treatment.

MSA has taken Mattie from her loving home and ripped our family apart. This is devastating to everyone involved. Including our sweet Mattie, our lovable goofball who doesn't understand any of this but is wondering what she did wrong to end up in a kennel torn from her family and everything she knows. It's this image that haunts me. Mattie is innocent and in true MSA fashion they are using her as leverage as they routinely do with their dogs.

Please sign our petition to urge MSA Security to return Mattie to the family who loves her.

And please let MSA and its CEO Glen Kucera know how you feel about this! Direct contact has a positive impact.

MORE INFO:

You can follow our story on Facebook: "Bring K9 Mattie Home" https://www.facebook.com/SaveK9Mattie/

And if you wish to contact us about anything, we do our best to answer each one of you individually and as promptly as possible through our email address: k9mattie@yahoo.com

Thank you all for your support, and God bless xoxo"

MORE INFO: FREEDOM SUPPORT ALLIANCE

YOUR SUPPORT MAKES FREEDOM POSSIBLE

FSA's goal is to promote the overall well-being of wartime allies by providing support, hope and a system designed to provide financial independence. After years of service and sacrifice, military interpreters have risked not only their lives but also the lives of their families to defend American freedom.

Whom it serves: Wartime allies, military interpreters, their families and Special Immigration Visa (SIV) recipients.

How it serves: Provide relief services, humanitarian aid, and partnerships with community resources and service organizations

Contact Info – Address:

    4011 W Sahara Ave. Suite 5

    Las Vegas, Nevada 89102

SÉAMUS Ó FIANGHUSA (FENNESSY)

Email: info@fsanv.org

Website: www.freedomsupportalliance.org

AUTHOR REVIEWS

"An excellent book - the author has great enthusiasm for his subject, and it comes through loud & clear when reading it. His style is easy to read and conversational - it's as though he is speaking directly to you."

— **R. BRUCE CRELIN**, *author of* The Great War and the Golden Age of Hollywood Horror *on Séamus' best seller* Heaven Help Us, Now!

"Sergeant Fennessy, you know all about this history"

— **PETE HEGSETH**, *Fox News host, author of Modern Warriors, and army infantry officer.*

"Séamus is one of the smartest and toughest SOBs ever…, oh, and he can sing too"

— **BRYN REYNOLDS**, *Séamus' Platoon Sergeant in Afghanistan, retired police captain, and successful artist (www.darkmountainarts.com).*

"[Séamus] needs a battlefield commission. Seriously, he is either the new CG [Commanding General] or his chaplain"

– **J.R.S.**, *former West Point professor and historian at the U.S. Army Center of Military History.*

"Very well spoken, on track, and level headed. We need some more of this and less hysteria!"

– **B. COLLINS**, *Afghan War veteran.*

"Great NCO, honest man, with a massive intellect on world/military history"

– **J.J. FALVEY**, *one of Séamus' former soldiers.*

"My mullah brother! You are the only good mullah I know"

– **"HK,"** *veteran Afghan American interpreter for U.S. Army Special Forces (Green Berets).*

ABOUT THE AUTHOR

Séamus Ó Fianghusa (Fennessy) is a bestselling author, publisher, and scholar who has been dubbed "the historian of the Fighting 69th" by Fox News. He is also a life-long devotee of Christian saints, such as St. Jude and St. Patrick, and has extensive expertise in problem solving through prayer.

He was a contributor to the groundbreaking Smithsonian Channel documentary *Fighting Irish of the Civil War*, and has been interviewed about the end of the Afghan War by numerous media outlets in the U.S. and in Ireland.

He is also an army infantry veteran with over 20 years of military service, 10 of which were with the legendary Fighting 69th. Séamus' combat experience was the subject of *Dúshlán*, the first ever Irish language documentary filmed in the Afghan war zone.

Séamus has earned respect for his vocal ability – first and foremost, in the service of God as a church cantor. He is a devoted practitioner of traditional Gaelic song. And for years, he has energized the *esprit de corps* of his fellow soldiers by singing songs in the Irish rebel tradition, both in training and in war.

In the private sector he worked as an Explosive Detection Canine Handler in New York City. A campaign to rescue his bomb dog, "Bring K9 Mattie Home," has garnered widespread attention and support.

He is a passionate advocate of traditional Gaelic culture, and has an especially strong loyalty to his adopted townland of Bun a' Leaca in the parish of Gaoth Dobhair, Tír Chonaill (County Donegal), Ireland.

As a historian, soldier, and Irish language activist, Séamus has been featured on a variety of media outlets internationally, including CNN, NBC, and Fox News in the United States, and RTÉ, TG4, and BBC in Ireland.

Heaven Help Us, Now!, Séamus' recent book about St. Jude, patron of lost causes, was the Amazon #1 Best Seller in Christian Saints and #1 New Release in Spiritual Warfare.

Made in United States
Troutdale, OR
10/25/2023